# The Fool's Poems
# Part I

## Honouring Our Brokenness and Happiness

## Wasyl Nimenko

### Goalpath Books

I0026869

Published by Goalpath Books 2021


The Fool's Poems Part I
Honouring Our Brokenness and Happiness


Copyright © Wasyl Nimenko 2021

The right of Wasyl Nimenko to be identified as the author of this work has been asserted in accordance with the Copyright, Designs and Patents Act 1988.

All rights reserved. No part of this publication may be reproduced, stored in a retrieval system, or transmitted in any form or by any means electronic, mechanical, photocopying, recording or otherwise, without the prior permission of the publishers.

ISBN 978-1-908142-627

Wasyl Nimenko was born in Ipswich, England. His mother was from Tubbercurry in the west of Ireland, his father from Dnipropetrovsk (now Dnipro) in central Ukraine. After studying medicine in London from 1974-1979, he began training and working as a psychiatrist. He worked at the 2,200 bed St Bernard's Hospital *(previously known as the 'Hanwell Insane Asylum' and the 'Hanwell Pauper and Lunatic Asylum')* but left psychiatry because of the overemphasis on the chemical causes and treatments of mental health problems.

He left psychiatry to train as a GP and a psychotherapist. From 1982 - 1991 he worked with survivors of torture. He worked independently, in the NHS, with the homeless and also with the emergency services and the armed forces.

In 1984 Wasyl Nimenko researched the stress of using virtual reality for Xerox among the first users of the Xerox Star, technology which has since become the standard in personal computers. In 2011 he carried out research into the use of archaeology in the psychological decompression of wounded soldiers, a service which is now available internationally to the armed forces as 'Operation Nightingale.' In 2013 he researched Post Repatriation Stress Disorder which was first described in 2015.

Although Wasyl Nimenko's professional activities have chiefly been in the UK he has also lived and worked in India, New Zealand and Australia. At present his main interest is in uncovering, recognising and realising our natural happiness.

## ALSO BY WASYL NIMENKO

### Non-Fiction

*Einstein and Ramana Maharshi*
*Uncovering and Recognising Awareness*
*Do you need a Doctor, Therapist or Guru?*
*Removing Our Delusion of Separateness*
*Carl Jung and Ramana Maharshi*
*The Spiritual Nature of Addiction*
*Acceptance and Meaning in Grief*
*Notes from the Inside*

### Fiction

*Invisible Bullets*

### Travel

*Searching in Secret India*
*Searching in Secret New Zealand and Australia*
*Searching in Secret Orkney*

### Poems

*The Fool's Poems Part II*

# CONTENTS

OUR PLACE IN THE WORLD

# OUR RESPONSE TO THE WORLD

In Japan there is an art form called Kintsugi. Sometimes it is used when someone seems broken by loss. They may repair broken pottery with gold dust in the glue so all the breaks are visible. The gold cracks show that when repaired with all its scars visible, the imperfect piece of pottery may be more beautiful than the perfect original. It can be a restorative process representing a changed perspective, of healing and wholeness.

The Fool also represents our journey to see our true self. The Fool has simple faith in the Universe and is unaware of the hardships and pain they will experience on their journey. During their journey the fool becomes aware of their ignorance, sheds their ego and is transformed by finding happiness inside.

# OUR PLACE IN THE WORLD

# 1. ANIMALS

## Comparative Consciousness

When cats are still with their eyes open and awake
Are they just being still?

I ask because they seem to be
And they seem to be able to be still better than us.

## Cats and Dogs

It is not that I don't socialise so much with humans,
It's just that birds have a sweeter song.
A dog unconditionally turns up to be stroked.
A cat is honest about purring.

A cat will be with you;
A dog will stay with you.
They both miss you a
And they welcome you back.

## Specialised

Flying, swimming and hibernating are for the eagle,
Shark and bear
Whilst our speciality is to think,
But what is it for?

Not just to compete, survive or just to stay alive.
Not to build and create
So perhaps it is for consciousness of happiness of being.

## Rescue Cat Trust Restored

She was thrown out and abandoned on the street
With her five kittens.
Seen struggling she was picked up by the cat rescue home.
There for eighteen months, rejected, not wanted,
Passed by every day by everyone who wanted a cat.

Then we saw her.
Her attitude was unfriendly, maybe even bitter and resentful,
On edge, probably wounded by beatings,
But shining through she was still her own self, with dignity.

One year after hiding everywhere, always hyper-vigilant,
She suddenly refused to be alone.
Everywhere you went inside or outside
She was there for company, affection.

Her hyper-vigilance gone,
She sits curled up anywhere, right now on a chair.
A small bowl of water, milk in the mornings then out for mice.
In the evening back in for company and purring.

If she was a human, her trauma would have caused PTSD
She would have become addicted to alcohol or drugs,
Had medication, therapy but instead she was restored,
Cured and healed by kindness, and being part of our family.


## Perhaps

It cannot be disputed that it is a lonely life
Not just for us but for animals too.
It cannot be disputed that everything is moving
And is part of life in some way.
It cannot be disputed that animals may also think about this.

## We are Not the Only Consciousness

We are not the only form of consciousness
Responding to stimuli
Which can mean life or consciousness.

Flowers and animals don't want to die.
Flowers and animals may worry about when they will die.
The planet may also worry about when we will die.


## Kindness

Kindness is treating someone
How you would want to be treated.
Animals show kindness, so it is not unique to humans,
But many of us choose not to be kind.
Receiving kindness can make the biggest difference
In someone's life.

Kindness can restore our belief in mankind,
Change our world view,
See that there are decent people
And this can give us a purpose in life,
That we have something we can pass it on.


## The Smallest Things

It's the smallest things we do which tell someone about us.
The smallest things we do say what we are.
It can be a card, the x for a kiss or a smiley face at the end
Looking you straight in the eye.
A bar, a purr, a stroke a smile,
An early morning surprise. A cup of tea can be enough,
Or just waving an extra goodbye can make it that special day.
The smallest things that we do which are the most important.

## Love and Affection Now

Cats and dogs help us mostly in one single simple way
As they help us stay in the present moment.

They don't live in the past.
They don't live in the future.

They don't want to save up.
They want things now.

They don't delay affection.
They show it immediately.

They show their fear, their anger.
Their love is on their face and tail.

## Present but Hidden

Cats don't seem happy or sad as they seem
Either comfortable or looking for comfort.

We too desire our happiness and we look for comfort too.
But how many of us look for and find happiness,
Not knowing it is already here.

## Why

The question animals do not ask is why?
Maybe they see it as forbidden.
Perhaps they do know that they don't ask
Because sometimes they seem to know without asking.

## Wild Animal's Wisdom

Adaptive to everything
Seems to be the main quality of human thinking.
Most of all, man respects wisdom to do the right thing
And protect his own.
Some endure pain until death for an ideal or a friend.

But others enjoy committing genocide or torturing
To make an impression.
Despite final warnings of our lethal intake
Of food, drugs or alcohol
We can't override our own intelligence even until death.

How can this intelligence be so desirable
When it is our worst quality,
Not serving our interests as social animals?
When wild animals learn what we do,
They shy away from us and hide.
We may be wise to follow.


## Our Neurosis

Our neurotic traits,
Like the animals we force them on,
Are due to living like the animals we cage.


## The Mouse

When you think you have heard a mouse,
Everything else is put on hold,
Thoughts, feelings, everything in life for a mouse.

## Education

I've learnt more from homeless people about people
Than I have from scholars, professors, doctors, teachers,
Bankers and lawyers.

I've learnt more about people from straight forward people
Than I have from scholars, professors, doctors, teachers,
Bankers and lawyers.

I have learnt more from animals about people
Than I have from scholars, professors, doctors, teachers,
Bankers and lawyers.

## How Very Dull We Are

If you have not written about your cat,
Perhaps you think your cat is not interesting
Apart from its desire for food.
But look here at us, pretty much the same,
Our basic desires often changing the course of lives forever.

Not many cats have that degree of influence
Perhaps because they are only regarded as pets.
We do have influence
But only because we are regarded as human.

How very dull we are
To make ourselves seem so much more important
When compared with our cats
Who actually know they are superior.

## 2. EQUALITY

### We Don't Know

We can never know what goes on inside another person's head.
We don't even know what our next thought will be.
With little humility,
We speak as though we know others and ourselves.

Occasionally, an honest person who admits they don't know,
Makes us see most of what we say
Is based on our imaginings.

Others don't know any more than us,
Cannot predict their own behaviour or the weather.
How much happier just to know you don't know
Is to know happiness.

### A Bit Crazy

Sometimes I have to change where I sit,
Just to see if I am seeing things right
Or to see if moving will magically change them.

Perhaps this is when things need changing
And I can't see this yet,
But I sense that something is peculiar.

Maybe this is intuition trying to bring itself to my attention.
All I can do is follow my feet
And move to see a different position.

When I doubt this I think I'm a bit crazy but then If I was,
I'd be the last to know.
So doubt is my close friend who can also seem strange.

## Goalpaths

The path is none other than the goal.
The goal is none other than the path,
So you are at exactly where you are supposed to be.

Anywhere you try and go leads you back to right here,
On the path and at the goal.
They are not in different times in different places.

Knowing truth is seeing
You cannot gain what you already have.


## Equal

Very careful not to get anything wrong
To offend anyone's anxious traits in case they feel angry,
In case they don't like me.

Hey, you know, so what.
Can I do this for everyone my whole life?
Do they and I need to grow up? Do we need to move on?

Manners are essential
But I am not their servant, therapist or hired hand
Or stuck in any permanent role.
I am equal.


## Equally we are what we are

As conscious as we can be in this world is the same for all
But uniquely different for each of us.

There are different levels which we can reach
But we are all stopped by ourselves.

## Tigers

Why do we strive to be so conscious and fulfilled
But tigers don't?

Why do we need to have a reason to live
But tigers don't?

Why do we get attached to everything
But tigers don't?

Why are we unhappy?
But tigers aren't?

## Inner Governor

You know where to find me.
Well most of the time, even sometimes
When you looked like you might lose it.

Something seems to catch you just before you can't be caught.
Is this precision skill or an inner or outer guardian?

Not knowing, not believing and having no outer control,
How can anything be managed except from inside.

## Comparisons

What they have done is a full and balanced life,
Whilst what I have done seems more chaotic,
Blown by a different wind.

Taken far away and then back to where we all started,
We didn't compare notes
But we do compare now we are home.

## No Potential Future

The future is an illusion.
It never existed.
It will never exist.
Just like the past, the future cannot exist.

We have the potential to guess the future
Only if we use the ability to see what is already here,
But we can never see the future.


## The Same Minds but Different

Remembering Indonesian, Chinese, Indian, Brazilian saints,
Whether Hindu Christian Jewish Islamic or Buddhist,
Shows respect for the lineage of what we see.

But what all of these uncover
Is to see we see the same.
We have the same body.

We want to be special in who we are.
We act the same in all our behaviours.
We each wish for happiness.

Like our fingerprints,
Our minds have different patterns
But we are the same.

# 3. KNOWING OUR PLACE

## Being True to Our Self

When we are jealous that someone may take our position,
Perhaps we can be generous with that person.
If they betray us,
Maybe it was meant to be that we were true to our self
Rather that the need for position.

## Criticism

We can think and then actually believe
That we are clever to criticise
Rather than look for the good.
Criticising inflates our egos full of hot air
Whereas looking for the good shows us what we are.

## Permanent Stillness

Since seventeen, when for the first time
I was able to be conscious in the peace and bliss of stillness,
Nothing has changed.

The world with its people, buildings and landscapes
Looks different on the outside but on the inside,
Everything is exactly the same in stillness.
It is good to know my place.

**I am touched**

I am touched by you asking when others would not penetrate,
When others would not ask,
When others would not express the sensitivity.


**Unstoppable Stillness**

Up in the cool slopes of the hills
And down on the sweltering plane
The unshifting sense inside is the same.

Unmoved but connected,
Detached but moved,
The heart is still beating with unstoppable stillness.

## 4. PRESENCE

### The Presence

There is a sense of being in the presence
Like in a temple or on a mountain.
When I peer at our mortality
I can see us coming and going through this life,
Walking but still,
Passed through in a flash and all this will be gone.
The landscape similar,
With new batches of us already coming and going.

### Vigilant Presence

Stillness keeps up its permanent vigilant presence,
Even when we sleep.

### Happiness is Inside

Are there sacred places which you can experience
To make you more yourself?

Where do you go when you want to hear someone
Inspire you so you can go inwards to help make you see?
Who do you go to?

When you want to be somewhere sacred
To make you feel in the presence of something greater,
Where do you go?

When you want to experience something
To make you more conscious,
Where do you go?

## Presence of Ancestral strength

Whenever you go away, even to distant lands,
It is only an apparent distance and time
Away from this heart and these hands.

The illusion of time, letting you see with different eyes
Because you are somewhere different,
Drops away when difficulties arise.

What has been relied on is tried
And when the strength from ancestors is summoned,
Inner decisions are resolved.

## Presence

There is an awareness of the intangible by our Inner self.
There is an awareness of the same intangible,
A presence in everything around us by our inner self.
This is presence.

## Present

For a while we are like a flower in bloom,
Full of our own colourful character
With our own singular marks of identification.
Our presence, briefly proud and unreproducible.
Then gone but forever present.

## Just Presence

What if I don't live?
What if I don't get a chance to see this?
Maybe it is just a presence I feel I won't see.

## Guesswork

How can you understand a presence
When you walk into a room?
Someone is just there.
Words cannot describe our consciousness.
Conscious of someone different,
We can only see what their consciousness
Does to our consciousness.


## The Power of Presence

Presence communicated effectively
Is more eloquent than words.
Presence is older than thoughts,
Older than words and lasts longer than words.
Thoughts captured just before they grow,
Recede and will go and let the self show.
Presence, a look, a glance, a sign,
A pause or a moment is more than any word.


## Where Is It?

When the statues have all gone,
All images put away,
Where is what is left of all that was our way?

It is not with the images
Which have all gone,
Or the thoughts which imagined them
But the self inside before the thoughts.

## Waking Up Happy

The presence of happiness at the start of a day
Cannot be compared.
Nothing matches it, seems like it or feels like it.
It can't get better
But it can carry on like the sun brightening everything.

## Our Presence

Perhaps all we can be is our presence.
Perhaps all we give and leave is our presence,
Not our words or deeds.
Perhaps all we can be is our presence.

## Absence

The brightest mind is not the person you relate to.
The strongest hand the most beautiful face
Are not the person you relate to.
The most deeply felt characteristic of someone
Is not what you see, what you hear or what you feel
But their presence.

## Dull Dull Dull

Dull we may look.
Dull we may act.
Dull we may seem,
But our dull thoughts only reflect our ego.
Not the presence of the shining brilliance
Of the inner light of the self.

## Spark of Fire

Fire as a spark of light,
Like realisation, the fulfilment of consciousness,
Is the one wishing being the many.

Fire as a spark of light
Is the energy behind the passions of love and anger
Behind creation and destruction.

Fire is the nature of our heart,
Of what never ends and never starts.


## Most Talk

All talk ends in silence
So why do we indulge so much in talk?
Is it a simple compulsion?

Perhaps we don't keep more quiet,
Thinking that talking is better than silence
Because talk is a release of nervousness.

In silence there is no nervousness,
Only the calmness of a mind disengaged.

In talk there is fear, friction, worry and many arguments
But there is great peace in silence.

Endless talking can avoid being here in silent presence.
In talk only words can be spoken
But in silence volumes can be communicated.

Words cannot express the power of presence
Spoken through silence.
All talk and words end in the stillness of silent consciousness.

# 5. MIRRORS

## Relationships

A good relationship is more than a mirror of yourself.
It is a mirror which not only talks back to you,
It kicks you hard and steps hard on your foot.

If you are unhappy without a relationship,
Having one won't always make you happy
Because you have to be happy to have one with yourself
Or a relationship will leave you.

To work,
Good enough relationships
Are like having a part time job,
They always need regular focused attention and effort.


## Rear View Mirror

When you become the person you criticised.
When you think the way they do,
The person you thought you were has gone.

You can only accept yourself or change.
You can turn your back on what you became,
Stand up, walk away and move on.

There is finding the centre again,
Finding what you really are
With not too much rear view mirror gazing.

## Mirror

Identifying with the sacredness of saint's faces
And with the spirit of sacred spaces is a mirror.

When we stop looking at personalities
And adornment our eyes are opening.

When all we see in the mirrors is our self,
What we see is naked and at last we are awake.


## Psychological Mirror

It is a surprise to suddenly see you've been trying
To appear like a different person, not who you are.

It is a surprise to suddenly see you've been trying
To appear like a smarter person, not who you are.

It is a surprise to suddenly see you've been trying
To appear like a helpful person, not who you are.

It is a surprise to suddenly see you've been trying
To appear like an honest person, not who you are.

It is a surprise to suddenly see you've been trying
To appear like a sorted out person not who you are.

It is a surprise to suddenly see you've been trying
To appear like someone else, not who you are.

**In the Mirror of the Self**

You kept on trying to fool me
In so many different ways,
And you nearly fooled me
As the distractions were never ending.

But your game had to have an ending. It couldn't be kept up.
It wasn't me I saw in the mirror
Because the collection of thoughts pretending to be me
Is not who I am.


**My Smile**

A smile when passing someone
Who has no connection or interest in you,
Apart from giving you a smile, can't be bought.

A smile from a much older or younger person,
Who you pass by may be the best smile you ever get,
That stranger's smile you can't forget.

Why is that particular smile so important?
Maybe it's like a mirror reflecting an inner sedated part of us,
We love but can't express.

Maybe that smile is our known but hidden potential inside.
Us in full bloom, spread fully open like full consciousness.


**Turning Inwards**

Hearing all the songs, all the music, all the poetry,
All the stories in all the books,
Point the way to being our inner self, which is there all along.
Perhaps they are mirrors.

## How We Look

We read to find out about a story
But we are looking for our story.
We don't know we are not reading but looking for a mirror.

## Another Way of Looking at It

Sometimes it's better to avoid the intellectual
And see things in emotional and physical ways.
Things can be seen in other ways by refusing to see them
As others expect you to or as you think you should.
Look in a mirror or at their feet.
Look at the breathlessness and see what comes in its silence.

## Reflection

Breath is not life.
It is what is behind it which makes and maintains life.
It is not the lips, the mouth which speak,
But the reflection of what is within.

Similarly, the mind is a mirror reflecting a light inside
But the mind is not the actual source of the light.
The mind is only a piece of kit doing a job.
The source of the light produces the mind.

# 6. ILLUSION OF THE EGO

## There is

There isn't nothing

## Artificial Intelligence

If you write down two thousand thoughts over a year or two,
You see your ego has an endless appetite
For taking up time and for seeming important
When it is only an electrical circuit on autopilot.

It is artificial intelligence
Because it is not real.
Real intelligence is consciousness
Without all the thinking.

## Our Life

What our life looks like to me is being human
But heavily programmed by everyone
To think we are the ego, the collection of thoughts,
Instead of the beautiful happiness inside.

## Putting on the Mask

Monday mornings are blank until I get in the car,
Then the scary part begins.
I look at what I could face today and I have to let it happen.
The adrenaline kicks in when I find my doctor persona.
Then I find my doctor voice and I detach and watch.

## Brain Hard Drive

I say I am anxious about later today
But what actually is the I that is anxious?

Is it the collection of thoughts and memories
Like information in a folder on a hard drive called Ego?

The thoughts are collected in electrical circuits
In binary form electronically
Or chemically and electrically in our brain.

Who identifies them or denies them?
That observer is the self.

## Humility and Modesty

Deceived by our own creation the ego,
An illusion just composed of thoughts,
We make a case for it and justify its importance
Rather than be humble and modest.

## Awards

Awards should decorate someone's life.
Awards should punctuate their efforts.
Awards should encourage others.
If there were none perhaps these aims would work.

Awards and medals do not decorate the fallen or the workers
But the privileged.
Those who keep us sane don't need medals to keep going
Because they keep going by being true.

## No Rest until the End

Finding the self and being the self has no end
Whilst the body is alive.
The body's functions fool us into thinking we are just the body.
Intelligently and with commitment it does its job.

There is a limitation as it cannot get behind what it thinks it is
Because thinking is limited by thinking.
Being conscious is not thinking.

## Inner and Outer Journeys

Getting on with people who you have to journey with
Until you decide to get off is choosing.
We choose how much of our time we are in the world
Or in solitude, detached from things of the world.

## Painless

Thoughts are painful.
They are not what we are told they are.
Without them we are happy, our true self.

## Ignorance Gone

When there is nothing more to break down,
There cannot be further suffering
Because there is no one to suffer.
There is no fear of death
As everything has already been relinquished.

## Happiness is Nothing

To be happy you need nothing, to be happier you need less.
To be happiest you need the least,
To be happy you need nothing.


## For Certain

There is no desire for happiness without suffering first.
Just when you think you have turned inside
Because you have suffered enough,
You may begin suffering four times more.

This is only the beginning of turning inwards
Which repeats itself every day,
Seeming to get unbelievably worse to make sure
There is nothing to turn outwards for.

There is no price for happiness.
Everything has to go.
What you thought was you is devoured.
Everything has gone except happiness.


## Un-negotiable

You cannot negotiate with the Self
Just as you cannot negotiate with God.


## Suburbia

I am not a suburban animal with walls to threaten me,
To tick boxes for my food.
I would rather be in the wild foraging or begging for my food,
Which is what the world is.

# 7. INFLUENCE

## What You Do

I don't miss the life I used to have.
I don't miss the well known people
But I do miss the honesty I saw in their hearts
When I saw what they could secretly do to help.

## No Change

Money cannot change what you are
But it can shine a light on you
Which can darken what is seen.

## Please Object

I don't object to what I've said or done
But I hope you object because that challenges it,
Maybe improving it.

## Changing the Wind

All the effort trying to change people is like changing the wind.
It can't be done, only the wind changes itself.

## We Can Show Only By Example

There is nothing better we can say or do
Than living by being an example.

## Tunnel of Light

Sometimes we go to the wrong end of the tunnel
To look for light
Which is always at one end.
We can think we are looking for it
But we can't see we are searching out the dark.


## Amplify the Positive

The more you work towards the positive,
The more detached you become from the nature of negativity.
Eventually you get so detached from negativity
That it is impossible to be in the same place.


## The Happiness of Ignorance

We don't know when our luck will run out,
When we then say to ourselves, 'Rotten luck.'
Knowing we don't know is a blessing
As knowing would be a tragedy destroying our happiness.


## Top Secret Gossip

If you have a conversation.
If you see a doctor or a lawyer,
Don't say anything important
Because there is no such thing as confidentially
In any of the worlds you see.
The only secure one is the one in you which doesn't gossip.

## Inspiration

The most inspiring thing is not another person.
It is not a place I love.
It's not a book or a film.
The most inspiring thing is not what someone said.
It's not a poem of play.
It's a blank piece of paper,
Like the self.


## All of Us

I saw a woman today who was like most men and women,
Uncomplicated, straight forward,
Friendly, kind and hard working.


## Carrying On

The only way to carry on is to be polite.
Calmness, patience and careful listening,
Especially silently, say more than words.


## Where Happiness Is

Strive for nothing because in nothing is the fullness of stillness
And in the fullness of stillness is happiness.


## You Are Your Choice

If you mix with people you can become like them
Or they may become like you.
You can choose to be with certain people
But don't forget how you are influenced is your choice.

## Leaving

We think our children are leaving us
But feelings, attachment and memories
Reinforce that this is not true.
Our children do not leave us.
We are going our own way finding all the things
We have reflected on
As we leave them.

## 8. PLACES

### Yet

Places stay but we must go.
Perhaps places let part of us stay
In a consciousness we don't yet know.

### Travel

We travel to find unknown lands,
Interesting people with stories
But what we do is travel to find our self
To find our own inner story.

### Mountaineering

We don't climb to conquer mountains only to know our self.
We shouldn't climb to conquer anything
Only to know our self.

## 9. SEARCHING FOR HAPPINESSS

### Get Out of Your Way

What we all want is the same,
It's just how we get it that's different.
We all want to be able to make ourselves happy with no pain,
To be happy about everything with no painful thoughts.

We get in our own way.
We sometimes blame this on others but whichever way,
It is our thoughts which get in our way,
So find out how to get them out of the way.

When you point your finger at someone,
Remember to look below at the other fingers on your hand
And see there are three fingers
Pointing back at you.

### Inspired Desire

What inspires me most is pain.
Yes pain, then the desire to not have it.
Pain makes me desire the happiness I know is inside,
The most powerful inspired desire.

## 10. TURNING INSIDE

### Eternal Internal

Externalisation of our thoughts,
Externalisation of our dreams,
Externalisation of our desires,
Externalisation of our happiness,
Externalisation of our self
Are in the opposite direction of happiness.

### Turning Inside

Wherever you go in your mind
You always come back to one thing,
Conscious of just being happy in stillness.
Awareness of just this with no thoughts is your natural default,
But relentless conditioning as you grow up
Obscures and eventually hides it.

You can imagine or believe your happiness is outside you,
Until enough suffering and pain brings you to your knees
And your ignorance is removed,
Leaving you only one place to turn, inside.

### Turning Around

Just before I see anyone and am with them,
I turn inwards and I try and turn off my thinking,
To let myself just be.
I have to close my eyes or put my hands or feet together
To help me turn inwards to be my self.

## Selfish

Sometimes I only seem to have one interest
Which is being happy inside.
Everything outside is only there to support this one thing
Which is about the self.
The self was there before my thinking,
Before I could see, hear or sense anything.
It is this that I am all about, not the part of me that thinks.
It is not selfish as it is to be shared.


## Insomnia

Suffering makes your mind overwork
And you cannot sleep for thinking.
Only when you are exhausted sleep arrives but is short.

It feels like it is never ending,
It is painful, strong, even overwhelming,
But it is only the mind and body which are overwhelmed,
Untouched is the inner self.


## Perfection

Every moment of consciousness, every thought and feeling,
Every movement and interaction
Are perfect as they are meant to be.


## A Single Home

There is always a need to look in.
We can't look out without looking in.
There is no journey unless it starts within,
So we should always be within.

## Impossibilities

Have you ever seen someone lift a happy cat up by its tail?
Have you ever seen the best swordsman use his sword?
Have you ever seen a happy rich man?
Have you ever seen inside?

## Only Being Now

Our Time is only now.
We think it will be longer
But it can only be now.

Our time is perceived sentimentally
As what we have been and what we have left,
But it can only be now.

Our time becomes other people's time
As we see we are handing over the baton in our relay,
But it can only be now.

## Being Poor

If you try to live thinking that money can make you happy
Because money can let you have things,
Do things and be things,
You may live long enough to see you are poor
Because all you have is money.

## Being Conscious

How clear to see we are only our nature,
What we say, write or do
Are only the results of our mind's activity.
But our nature is just being conscious.


## Inability to Stay Still

Returning to see you have been thinking and not being still
Is the return to consciousness from reduced consciousness.

Our inability to stay with being still is our greatest weakness,
Being still our greatest treasure.

Thinking subtlety loosens our grip
And off we go on another tangent of thinking
Until we return again, seeing we have been thinking,
Not being thoughtless.

Being still is our permanent nature,
Thinking our temporary interrupter,
Just as dark appears necessary for light.


## No One

I know what happens at the end
But what is going to happen to me next?
Me is just a collection of thoughts.
Me doesn't exist so who does what happen to?
Perhaps nothing happens to no one?

## Freedom

The relief of not having to know anything.
The relief of not believing in not being good enough,
Allows happiness to flourish within.

The satisfaction of seeing the rewards of suffering.
The practice of the presence of humility,
Opens us to freedom through surrender.


## When It Doesn't Work

When you cannot write,
Usually life is showing you
It is more important than writing
And is what you may need to write about.

When you cannot draw,
Usually life is showing you
It is more important than drawing
And is what you may need to draw about.

When you cannot sing,
Usually life is showing you
It is more important than singing
And is what you may need to sing about.

When you cannot meditate,
Usually life is showing you
It is more important than meditating
And is what you may need to meditate about.

When you cannot be still,
Usually life is showing you
It is more important than being still
And is what you may need to be still about.

## Fighting for Peace

My father would have loved the new country he was in.
A refuge, an escape from the lethality where he was born,
Which I have heard from him and others from elsewhere
But not seen.

How do we keep safe from what will be repeated?
How can we?
We can only keep safe if we become involved in it,
Being part of the whole process of fighting it.

## Shocked to Make the Effort

Too much pain and suffering eventually turn us inwards,
To find the special place where happiness is.

We align with our inner self,
Using solitude, detachment and our attitude.

Through silence, meditation, enquiry and surrender,
We begin our aim.

Our aim is removal of ignorance to be happy in stillness,
Which is already our truth.

Basically, shock changes us inside to make the effort,
So we can embrace inner happiness.

## Today

Today is the only day you will ever be
With no reminders from the past,
No thoughts or the future
Because you can only be conscious now.

## All Else Second

What has influenced me
Is someone who tried to find themselves
In the time they had,
With as much effort as a drowning person gives to breathe.
All else is second.


## Thinking Thief

What is behind us and in front of us
Stops us being where we are within.
Why can't they say it in school?
Why don't they tell us?
Why aren't we taught the truth that happiness is within?

It's because of fear that we would be happy,
Fear that we would not be interested in the world,
Fear that we would be detached from the world and
Fear that we would have all we need


## Fear of Unhappiness and Turning Inwards Now

Fear can be of everything in the future.
When we stay with what we are now,
Fear cannot exist in the present.

Desire can be for everything in the world.
When we turn our desire for happiness inwards
We are given everything.

## Just Being Still

We have not lost the ability to turn inwards
To find our inner stillness.
We have just been programmed
To think all the time, instead of just being still.

## Just Being Stillness

Freedom is always ours to be what we are,
But we mistake what we could be for what we are,
Chasing our freedom further away.

## From Suffering to Cure

Writing about what cannot be written or described in words
Is vital to understand it.

What cannot be described properly, adequately with words
Has to have more help to be seen.
Seeing it is understanding so it can be experienced.

To experience something it has to be encountered,
But first you have to know about it.
You have to be looking because you desire it.

To desire it you already know it exists.
To get there you could follow someone who has been there
But they are so difficult to find.

Some will have left a trail of words you can follow
Outlining the path they took,
Only so that you can find your path easier.

## Unaffected

A thousand years back or forwards
Our brains like the rest of our bodies
Have been changed by use.
The environment which we inhabit
Constrains or frees our mind's adaptation;
Our consciousness unaffected.


## Idealism

The tenderness of words, forms or sounds we leave behind
May not reflect what we are.
They may reflect the opposite of what we are,
Only our idealistic thinking.


## Always Already

You cannot arrive at where you already are
Unless you don't sleep and don't forget.

You cannot become what you already are
Unless your life gives you so much pain.

You cannot acquire what you already have
Unless your life gives you so much suffering.


## Other than Being Itself

It can almost seem to drive us to the truth,
Trying to find out why we are here.
What if any meaning does our consciousness have
Other than being itself, our self.

## As We Are

Oh blank sheet of paper
Why has it become normal to try and change you?
Oh thoughtless mind, why can't I leave you as you are?
Where has this come from?
Why can't we just be as we are?

We can't be more important than we are.
We can't be happier than we are.
We can't become anything.
We can only be as we are; nothing else.

## Last Words

The transient consciousness we have;
The sense of consciousness we know is us,
Is the last aspect of us we have to let go of
Before its complete surrender.

## We see by seeing what we are not

I have a body which is part of me but is not what I am.
I have thoughts which are part of me but are not what I am.
I have feelings which are part of me but are not what I am.
All I can know I am is consciousness.

## 11. NATURE

### Never

If you respect yourself, you can't disrespect anyone.
Nature may make errors but is never indifferent.

If you are compassionate with yourself,
You can't be cruel with anyone.
Nature may make errors but is never cruel.

If you are simple with yourself,
You can't be complicated with anyone.
Nature may make errors but is never complicated.

If you are honest with yourself,
You can't be dishonest with anyone.
Nature may make errors but is never dishonest.

### The Great Book

The Great book the greatest of all to read
Is the one that is in front of you, around you all the time to see.
She shows you rather than tells you all you need to know,
From how things are formed and how things grow.
She shows you death in all its ways.
She shows you minerals, animals and plants
And shows you how to the sun they dance.
The greatest book is Nature herself,
Silent, roaring, weak and strong,
Teaching and showing us all lifelong.

## Copying nature

You cannot cheat nature. You cannot cheat life.
It has its way of balancing
Because balance is its nature, worth copying.
The best art, the best architecture, the best relationships
Try and copy nature, being and looking the best.


## Thread

There is a thread
Which we all have as the golden thread of life itself.
It may connect to your partner, to an ancestor, a friend,
To a memory or to hope.

The thread which connects everyone to make everything,
Even the intangible is the thread,
The cord which is not cut at birth
But woven as instructions deeper than our genes.


## Not Knowing When to Stop

Nature does not always behave how we would expect.
It can kill itself by destroying what it lives off.

It can be overgrowth,
Not knowing when to stop.

It seems to have more feedback loops to encourage it
To feed, to grow and to replicate than to stop,
Which includes us.

## Our Nature

We are given our share of what is nature.
What we do with it is our nature.


## So Just Be You

It's easy to be complex, difficult to be simple,
Easy to be natural, so be you.
It's hard to be right and easy to be wrong
But being right has more potential, so be you.


## Too Early

We were told to start with,
That life doesn't seem fair.
Every sense bursting with activity
Like a garden in full spring.

Soon the last days will arrive.
Yes autumn is passing.
We can all say this because
It seems like a very long life at the beginning.
But then we are surprised when we realise
That it will be over soon and we will have to leave.

We carry on and start getting ready,
Realising there is nothing to be which we haven't been,
Nothing to do which has been left undone,
Nothing to say which hasn't been said,
Nothing to see which hasn't been seen.

## Above All

Sometimes we don't know what has brought us to this place,
But we usually see it if we keep looking.
Perhaps what has brought us here
Wants to show something inside us,
Which is not just about thinking,
And is what we trust above all else.


## Struggle of Fairness

Fairness strongly suggests something
Bound by rules and standards,
But life in the outside world is not so well organised.
Animals are naturally wild; people steal, kill
And destroy the land they live on.
A struggle with these is a struggle with nature,
Which may not be won.


## Above All Else

Trying to find resonance with someone
Reflects lack of stillness of oneself
Returning to stillness is our origin and fate.
Stillness is never early or late.
Above all thinking at the end is inner stillness.
Above all religion at the end is inner stillness.
Don't listen to anyone.
You have to listen to your self to find your inner stillness.
Above all is your own inner stillness.

## Invisible Cloud of Stillness

When there are no more words, I am not dead.
Senility has not arrived,
A stroke has not occurred, but even if so, there is peace.

It is nature taking its place,
Its time in its space,
In stillness as others grow in my place.

There is no competition as nothing can be done.
The invisible cloud of stillness
Silently takes over everything and everyone.


## Precious

Am I precious about my inner state?
It is precious to me?
Maybe not to you or anyone else,
So to me I can't be too precious.


## Our Natural State

Our nature is happiness so why can't we have it?
It is unconditional happiness because it is always there,
But accessing it is conditional on being our self.


## What We Are Given

There is no other,
No next, only this
Which is what we are.

**No More Left**

There is no more time available or wanted,
No more opportunities;
Reality of truth suddenly becomes everything.


**Not Precious**

Not enough value is placed on the inner self.
We encourage people to sacrifice it
To industry, to society, to lack of stillness.


**Exercise and Sport**

Exercise is natural and good for you,
But sport is manmade and can be dangerous.
There is nothing wrong with exercise or sport
But sport can injure you.

Exercise is a calming measured regulator,
But sport can be so competitive it can lose its way
And become aggression.


**Our Natural Desire**

We might have seen the happiness
We expected from the outside world doesn't last,
And so we may have already started searching
For the happiness we know is inside us.

Life for many of us may have been difficult,
So chaotic and so traumatic
That we still suffer and turning inside is our only refuge.
Happiness is our nature and finding it is our main desire.

## Inwards

The aim of turning inwards
Is to find the happiness of inner stillness.
When stillness is found it is our truth.

The tools we need to turn inwards
Are to be detached from the things of life with a quiet mind,
Whilst being fully in the middle of life.

What we need to do with the tools is to
Simply enquire into our nature
And completely surrender to our nature by being still.


## Boring

Life is never boring but it may seem so
If our mind is disturbed or perturbed.

The most complete complex activity of our whole being
Is consciousness.

Exploring it, being it is blissful but could not be boring
Unless you are disturbed or perturbed.


## Unfocused

My head goes into a spin from too much driving around
With no focus in sight.
Eventually, my eyes become unfocused,
Then the inner balance needs trusting.

## Flowers

Flowers are colourful messengers
Trumpeting and displaying
That their fragility and short life are our shared state.

## The Underground

There is always an underground group of heavies
Who use muscle or psychological muscle,
Working for people at the top of every organisation.

Countries, religions, farmers and shops.
How else would they get their dirty work done?

## Chance

We have assumptions that our world is stable,
That people are predictable
And everyone is doing what they should do.

How wonderful it might be in such a pleasant state
To see it like this.

Then accidents, chance meetings, fatigue, forgetting
Or remembering place us where we didn't expect to be,
And finally we see.

## Bare Essentials

For all our technology
The sun, wind and sea support life the most
And are our essentials.

## The God We Seek We Are

When we surrender to our nature we do a curious thing,
As most of us surrender to God, because our nature is God,
We surrender to out self.

When we conjure up an image of God,
It is from inside our self,
So it has to be an image of what is already there.

If it is an image of what is already there,
What is already there inside us
Is God.

So when we surrender to our nature
We surrender to our God, which is our self,
Name it what you want.


## The Best Pilot

In full flight
Ready to change in an instant, ready to stop, ready to continue,
Keeping the main aim the main aim,
The best pilots are birds.


## To Seek and Find

Plants expand to their limit everywhere they can go,
Not stopping at blocks but repeatedly try to move.

We try and do things we can't and keep on
Trying, challenging and struggling to expand ourselves.

It is a quality of nature to do this persistently,
To seek and find without end, leaving all else behind.

## Stroke

Someone's thinking can turn from
Sensible to unintelligible noises in an instant.
It's not that it could happen, it happens with a stroke.

It can change us into a dependent person
Who now needs total help,
But we only hear and see the fringes
Of what has to be done for someone like us.

Burdens which are not ours are not easy to even imagine,
Just as not knowing them is a freedom
Some can remember as bliss.

## Blossoming Birthday

It's the first day of another year,
A new year's day.
Like daffodils and tulips trumpeting in spring,
Today trumpets in how young you are.

Like all the flowers
We too as children of the Universe must age,
And in ageing we blossom and give much, so others
Can see the beauty we are, which we never knew we were.

## Troubles

Anything that moves is Trouble.
Anything that doesn't move is trouble.

## The Wake Up Call of Consciousness

Our consciousness is demoted to less importance
Than the transient happenings of daily life,
So that we are hardly aware of our consciousness.

Our consciousness is almost always
Pushed into the background
Which it is mostly ignored and forgotten.

It only becomes present when dreadful things
Happen to us or others
And our existence is threatened.

Bringing consciousness up to the surface
So it is with us much more and more frequently,
Is the beginning of inner work.

## Too Straight

Sophistication is debasing nature
And that is why nature has no straight lines.
Forces form left and right making swerves and curves
Which may result in going in the same direction.

The straight line comes from man's sequential, logical thinking
And wanting to achieve progress.
Less progress is made with straight lines
Than with curves, swerves and circles,
Which is how all things grow.

## A Thousand Nights

Just over a thousand days
Three years looked back on,
Looks like three weeks or months.

Memory is not of time
But of people, places and things
Which having changed.

Just over a thousand nights
To emerge every morning,
Incredibly thankful to be conscious.


## Life's Peak

Completion of our biggest work is so satisfying
Because we achieve the best we can ever do.
We reach the top of the highest mountain
And we are radiant with happiness.

Why is there so much fear of completion
When with every step nearer there should be even more joy?
There should be increasing excitement
Knowing that we will achieve it then die.


## What You Do and Are

If you say you don't like what you do,
You put you down.
What you are during that time,
You put down you.

## No More Praying

We don't pray anymore
Because we don't believe in god
Because we think we are god.


## With praying gone

That part of our self does not disappear
And it still needs to be nourished.
For being god to be true, we need to use that knowledge
To be conscious and happy as only god can be.


## Respect for Nature

Just as we have some sense of the job we are doing,
As we begin bringing up our children,
We have about as much sense that our own life is wearing out.

Being conscious of these is not usual
Because it is not part of how we are programmed,
But comes sharply into focus the nearer the parting comes.

Like a beautiful flower
During a happy day,
The cycle has its nature which we respect.

## Counting

Numbers must exist in nature.
Nature must be able to count.
Not like we count by thinking but some other way.

How could nature be so accurate,
Without counting, without computing, calculating?
So nature can count.
If nature counts what else can it do?
It seems it can make things like you.


## Standard Operating Procedures

Manufactured programmed thoughts and behaviours,
Like formal over-manicured gardens,
Can leave you feeling as if we are becoming unnatural.
But perhaps it is just easier for us to be this way in the world.

## 12. TECHNOLOGY

### Tell Don't Show

If it were not for screens, the movies and computers
What would have happened to man?

What would have happened
To his story telling, to his myths, to his beliefs?

Would we still be telling stories
With words from a mouth, to an ear, to a heart and a mind?

I was there, I heard and I saw
What are now the myths and stories
That the media can only show but we can no longer tell.

### Digital Masters

These thoughts, these words
Are what comes when I am waiting
And are based around the first word which appears
Because I am not relaxing
Because of the screen where thoughts appear.
The technology pulls me in, pulls me away from other things
Away from the room,
The silence and from the walk in the field outside.

It has been days since I wrote the last line above this
Because I have been in the field walking.
I have been walking, which is better than doing this.
But this leaves a trace,
A record of how you can get drawn in to anything
When the task is to do what you came here for. It is a warning.

## Down and Out

Is man progressing, advancing and improving
With a better quality of life?

Are we as prosperous in that we are flourishing, thriving,
Happy, healthy and in a state of good fortune?

We are more competitive and less co-operative, less sharing
And we are more greedy,
More focused on celebrity not equality.

Parents teachers and priests have lost their influence
To psychology, technology and the New Age.

We are in a crisis about our core values
Which define us as civilised human beings.

We are over-immersed in virtual worlds,
Lacking authentic interaction with family, friends, nature
But mostly ourselves.

Binge use has substituted everyday experiences
So we can no longer survive without specialist training.

We can't be kind or gentle, relate or relax
Without specialist training.
We can't be conscious or even spiritual
Without specialist training.

Have we improved?
And become less superficial, higher more thoughtful people?

Just as all religions started at their peak
And are always in decline,
We are less flourishing, thriving, happy and healthy,
So more down.

We are superficial, looking less inwards,
We have gone from inside to being only out.
We are not interested in our highest state of happiness,
But have descended into the world of pleasures, more down.
We have become down and out.

## Currency

We have become obsessed by something which had value
But is now valueless.
How did we get rid of its value?
It has replaced food, generosity,
Kindness, help and compassion.
It is now digital, so completely valueless,
But it is still exchanged for time and for our life.

## Just Being

A group of men and women
Can achieve more than any machine, computer or technology
By being consciously happy.

## Wallpaper

There are no books here
Because books are officially now wallpaper.
What did they give? What will not be there?
They formed the bundles of knowledge on calfskins first,
Then on paper. Then on scrolls, bound and also in Brail.
What can be read on a stormy day?
What can be seen and understood which never decays?
Barehanded like Stone Age man under a naked sky,
Only those who have been taught
To think then write will survive.

## Luddite

Do I want any more modernity
To take me away from eternity?
Do I need more devices to inject me
With more information that doesn't protect me?


## Virtual Reality and Sacred Spaces

Computers eight hours a day might be worse
Than being down a mine because
Where we look for happiness has changed,
Because what we think is happiness has changed.

Foolishly our sense of our self is formed
By fishing for compliments in others opinions,
By numbers of followers
Rather than looking at ourselves and our own self-worth.

We are not born unhappy
But because the world makes us unhappy,
We look for happiness out there rather than inside,
Where it is hidden and can be uncovered.

Be a nerd be a geek, a loner, a recluse, an eccentric,
A drop out who cares not a jot what others think about you
Because you are happy.

Be abnormal and visit the wonder of a sacred site.
Go on a distant pilgrimage or a silent retreat.
Be a freak and meditate
Or contemplate being a spiritual person.

## Reading Maps

When technology goes wrong
And gives you the wrong directions,
You realise what we have thrown away.

A person sitting beside you reading a map
Is a warm person,
Not a tool of a voice presenting as help.


## Technological Communications

Your computer mimics what people used to do,
Telling you important information,
Answering your questions which can be helpful.

Your computer can tell you how you could be feeling,
How you should be feeling,
Even how you would have been feeling.

But it can't tell you what you are feeling
Or what you are thinking,
What your hopes are or your dreams.
It can only guess.

It can't change your level of consciousness
From remembering to wishing the future,
Or being happy or just being alive in the present moment.

What people used to do also included their presence,
A name with a history, opinions, attitude
And their passion to be here alive.

## Collection of Thoughts

My secret wish in writing is to empty my mind,
To drain it to permanent exhaustion,
So the hard drive will have nothing left in it
That is worth accessing and thinking about.

But the quiet mind will try to restart
The imagined collection of thoughts, the ego,
Which will tick over by itself,
Imagining the world it thinks it is.

## Warning, Ceaseless Technology

The essentials of daily living have become secondary
To the never ending tidal waves of demands
From interacting with technology.

Technology has pushed aside,
Almost taken away my attention and perception
Of simple things which keep me nurtured
Cleaning, cooking and being still.

That distance from what I recognise
Can be manipulated by technology
So it appears to be close
When it is getting further away.

Perhaps I have to become
So far away from what I remember or accept,
That warning bells ring to signal change must begin.

## The Latest Thing

Perhaps there are too many competing gas stations
To speed up cars driven by fast drivers,
In a society which needs drugs to sedate them at night.

The green fields were exchanged for money,
Now stored in the warehouses on the land by farmers,
Instead of used for growing food.

We invested in building more computers
Rather than planting bulbs to make future generations
Smile at the daffodils and be happy.

We invested in outer stimulation
Rather than turning back inside
By to singing, dancing, music, smells,
Exercise, chanting, and silence
Which turns people to go within.


## The Surrounding Skies

Shafts of bright light coming down from the sky
From the Aurora Borealis in the early evening,
Must have inspired stories of spirits in the sky.
It still does.

The power of the skies changed
When we started transmitting information
By radio, telephone, fax and the internet
And launched aeroplanes, missiles, satellites and rockets.

We could not do much better than reclaiming
The clean air of the skies,
Removing the pollution of signals and transport,
So our hearts and minds are free from them and at peace.

## 13. STRANGE PEOPLE STRANGE PLACES

### Arrivals

How you arrive is not important, it's what you arrive as.
Did you have a good stay and arrive in your own happy way?
Did you have happiness? Did you have pain?
Did you pass anything on? Has everything you had gone?
Are you happy to be here relieved all is done
Or did your life leave other people's lives undone?

As the graveyard keeper I let everyone in.
I've seen many after a fulfilled happy life
And the worst types from everywhere always want to arrive
As the richest person in the graveyard.

### Lizard Hand in a Crazy Land

The deep rhythms of the Aborigine digeridoo player
In the Sydney outdoor shopping mall vibrated in my heart.
The low note made the air vibrate my chest wall
Like it does with the deep note of a lion's roar
Or that same note from a church organ.

Not sitting together but also on the bench,
A white girl began swaying.
First she fell sideways and then forwards.
His deep notes got louder
As if trying to wake her from the needle's delivery.

Then she lost it and was falling
About to hit the concrete ground face first,
But between both was the lightening hand
That had just held the lizard carved
On the side of his digeridoo.

## Your Grave

Those rocks now lie behind the wall
Where we threw them when all five of us dug them up
Whilst digging your grave.

We moved them there after being there for thousands of years.
Slowly covered, drowned in the slowly forming peat
At one millimetre a year.

They were waiting for you ready to welcome you from a baby,
Through being a small boy, a strong man
To the death which brought you here.

After thousands of years they now lie behind that wall
In the sun with you in their old resting place,
Both now settled under the stars.


## The Royal Family

Freesias look special
And the smell better than their strange elegant looks.
The effects of inhaling their smell intoxicates.
The smell is difficult to compare except
With perhaps honeysuckle, jasmine, or a rose,
The rest of the royal family of all smells.


## Escapees

Orkney, the enigmatic isles of ancient things,
I remember the wind with hardly any trees,
Many called Scot and many pure Vikings.
Land of the lights, the burial places,
Tomb of the Eagles, the bones, the escapees.

## North Ronaldsy

The smallest of all the Orkney isles, you made me smile.
The birders and twitchers, the Kirk,
The pub with no beer or food.

The doctor selling fags and booze to his patients
Whilst claiming fees for running smoking cessation clinics
And the General Medical Council
Saying 'There is nothing unethical if he wants to.'


## Signs

It is difficult to be aware of signs.
The wrong ones always say, 'This Way.'
The right ones don't say, 'Not This Way.'


## Bookshop Armchairs

Do bookshops not have lounge chairs, arm chairs and sofas
Because standing up reading a book
Makes you want to sit and read it.

Maybe this option is deliberately removed
So the only way you can sit and read further
Is to buy the book, leave the chairless rooms
And go to a café or home.

## 14. OUR SECRET LIFE

### The Secret Life

Reactive to reality and to fantasy
Trying to sometimes marry the two to find which way to go,
We are this terrible beauty.

Unknown to most, spending more time in the spirit
Than the world or in the body,
Serving only that inner master, answers everything.

### Ignorance Removed

Life is experienced like watching a play
With a curtain in the way.
Vague movements can be seen and muffled sounds heard.

Our perception and our reactions with the curtain
Are strained to guess what is happening
Behind the curtain and its effect on us.

Removing the curtain,
All is understood, everyone appears silent
And there is stillness when all is seen.

### Self-Respect

My occasional outbursts of disclosure twice a year
Are better than the self-harm
Of keeping my own feelings inside
And not finding out how I am.
My heart is not on my sleeve as much as it used to be.
It is in my eyes.

## Desire

Desire can be anything but one thing it is
Which we are not taught is that it is a duty.
It is essential as food, shelter warmth and love,
The ability to enjoy our life, to be happy inside.

## Junctional Places

That divide on the shore between the earth and sea,
The sea and sky, the sky and earth
Is where the mystery could be solved
But is not permitted for its own sake.

On a boat the line between the boat and the sea,
The sea and the sky, the sky and the boat,
Is where the mystery could be solved
But is not permitted for its own sake.

These seemingly ordinary lines,
The meeting points of opposites
Keep us from the next level
Of the stars and beyond.

## Everything and Nothing

Maybe there is only the spiritual.
It is what we are here for.
It is what we are.
It is what we are doing.
It is what we are being.
It is where we are from, where we are and where we remain.
It is how you are nothing and everything.

## Still Deceiving

Dreams of being in India still grab me every day.
I've been in that dream, lived there but I still dream.
You still dream of someone,
A love but only in your dream land.
In the light of day you would still fall out.


## Outgrown

When I look at the things I have kept
And still keep from my daughter's childhood,
I feel slightly odd
As I try to work out why.

Some tiny shoes, small wellies, a coat and jacket
As small as my jacket pocket.
Dozens of her drawings from age four.
I keep them because photographs are not as real.


## Solitary Lives

We don't live isolated lives only lives of solitude,
But we aren't told this.
We have difficulty connecting to the things of the world
Because we think we are connected.
We are more separate than we think or we are told.


## Nothingness

I'm not afraid of nothingness and I hope you are not
Because what could be more pointless
Than painful nothingness.

## Glue-Force

What holds all the billions of stars apart and together
We know nothing about.
Words, maths and physics try to explain it
But it seems beyond human comprehension.
If this is the case we are no less
But it may be time to stop considering the consequences of this.


## The Spirit

There is nothing more important as it is everything about us,
What will be remembered about us,
What we take with us and leave behind.

Everyone is about it. Everything is about the spirit,
Our world, all the billions of stars,
The energy holding it all together is our spirit.


## Its Stillness

At first you can't see it and some never can,
But when you do see it, it is all you can see.
You say how could I have missed it
As it doesn't seem possible to miss?

The mountain in front of you means something,
But you can't quite say what.
It doesn't have a spirit.
It is the spirit.

It doesn't move at all in its stillness,
The same as our spirit
And that is why we find mountains
Are places of our spirit.

# 15. PROFESSIONALS

## Emergency Doctor's Attitude

Believe nothing anyone tells you and only half of what you see.

## Perils and Perks of the Job

At the end of a day,
The gardener can't quite get the soil out of his hands,
The banker the money from their mind,
The doctor the suffering they have seen in another's heart.

As a student I was pulled out of the outpatients
By the paediatrician.
He noticed my fear of working with children.

I said I was scared because babies couldn't speak, so he said,
'When you stop being worried, it's time to stop being a doctor.'

Children now still scare me but because
They carry knives after they have taken drugs.

Only the sick need doctors. That's why I carry on,
Perhaps to meet that parent
Whose child has that knife that's next a gun.

To show them why they think they need what they want,
Instead of what they can have, to let them see what they are.

**That Doctor**

That doctor helps you stop being your unhealthy you.
You are taken to another level, a new place which is also you,
So what the doctor has shown you is that you can change,
That you are different to what you thought.

Can you be shown other parts of you
Which you had not seen or thought of but might like to?
There is a choice because
First you have to want to hear, then you have to listen.

There is another choice because
You have to want to take the medicine,
Then you have to choose to actually take it.
Then you have to stomach it.


**Specialist Advice**

On my first day in accident and Emergency
Trevor the consultant said, 'Believe nothing anyone tells you
And only half of what you see.'

On my first day of Psychiatry Colin the consultant said,
'Don't worry there are only the mad, the bad and the sad.'

On my first day in paediatrics Hugh the consultant said,
'When you stop being scared of children you're dangerous.'

What would my advice be today?
'Your happiness trumps other's.'

## Scenes

They really believe I've not heard this scene before,
Twenty to thirty times a year. It is what I see,
But they are right, because
I've not heard them actually speak before.

The familiarity doesn't leave me feeling contempt,
Only sadness with the frequent reminders
That we treat each other with so little kindness.
I am disappointed that we don't improve with age
Or with generations of history.

The draining price of having to listen,
The pain of empathic listening,
Then the addicts impact already showing on her baby's face,
Always reminds me of the passion to help,
But of not being able to do anything.

The relief and joy of shutting the door on a difficult day's work,
The decompressing meditation on the way home.
There are many others whose day has tried them too,
Knowing the cycle must begin again at dawn,
So we can all meaningfully live and truly feel alive.

## Therapists

Too much therapy but no food in the cupboard.
Too much therapy but no job.
Too much therapy but no company.
Too much therapy but no respect for anyone.
Too much therapy but no inner happiness.

## Professional Moral Gymnastics

How do you run a church, or a school,
A police force, the armed forces or a country?

You ignore everything that is sacred.
You ignore everything you know.
You ignore everything that is right.
You attack all opposition for resources.

## The Farmer and the Fisherman

The farmers land is his to rule
With a cold heart and a hard hand.
Everyone and everything,
A slave to money with no visitors or guests,
Unless they pay
And all dogs shot if they stray.

The fisherman risks his life at sea, a servant to its weather,
Thankful for a lucky day.
Always sharing what belongs to no one,
Helping with no fee, all who pass.

The animals fed sludge in cages,
No grass beneath their feet, sun or touching hand.
Only before their sale for slaughter to clear their ringworm
Are they put out in the sunshine.

The fish have swum the seas for years
And freedom has been their lot.
Most will escape the net or rod,
Only a few are predestined for the pot.

## World Without Heart

Some want to understand as much as they can
To change what they can.
Some are happy with everything,
Knowing everything is as it should be.
Knowing is the path of the head,
Being is the path of the heart.
Medical education without a heart cannot heal or teach.


## Perils of Showtime

Many singers hate singing the same songs
Every night for decades.
They leap at the chance to cancel performing
To seek revenge on their choice.

Some musicians are not interesting
But can interest and
Stir the masses with their skills.

Some comedians try to be cheerful
Despite frequently being depressed.
They fight a cruel battle of having insight
That their jokes will never let them be happy.

Some actors can never be beautiful enough
Because it would threaten their belief
And the world of competitive Narcissism.


## Off Duty but On Call

Maybe this is just left over from the nature of what I do.
Perhaps it is me not being the professional
But relaxed off duty in the world on call to within.

## Elite

The best swordsman never uses his sword.
The best therapist rarely says a word.
The best thinking is not to think.
The best communication is silence.
The best vision is with closed eyes.
The best parent is the child.
The best day is today.
The best time is always now.
The best king doesn't rule.
The wisest thinker is the fool.
The best chef is your stomach.
The best doctor is you.
The best friend is you.
The best person to ask is you.
The best person to change is you.
The only person to change is you.


## Professional Unprofessionals

Doctors are perfectionists, who like the perfect death,
Whether by nature or by their hand of intervention.
Even killing in combat has to be perfect
So less time is spent treating casualties.

They can have indifference to supervising someone's torture
So that it can carry on being used to inflict pain
And display the naked reality of humanity.

Only doctors and psychologists still supervise torture,
To say if the person can have more
So that it can carry on being used as a calling card
Instead of banned forever.

## Conditional Work

It seems to be a condition that to be an accountant,
Your own money is in a mess,
If you are a doctor, you are not well,
If you are a dentist, you have bad teeth,
If you are a policeman, your hands are never clean,
If you are a builder, your house is falling apart,
If you are a cook, you are overweight,
If you are a teacher, you find it difficult to learn,
If you are a psychotherapist, your relationships are in a mess,
If you are happy, it's because you know suffering.


## Healing

What is this healing time that the physician
Knows of six weeks?
What takes place in the biblical forty days and nights?


## Good news

What wonderful news to hear
You are not going to be a scientist,
A one hemispheric binary thinking cog in a machine.
Instead your world is ready
To be drawn and painted by you
In forms and colours which have no words.
Books are now wallpaper,
Money is digital communication
Which has taken over respect for what is within.
Nothing can create from inside except us.

## The Doctors Office

Industrialised medicine delivers doctors nurses
And administrators
Who are unconcerned beyond being at fault,
Unconcerned with your inner dialogue or outcome.

It would make no difference to them whatever your request,
Whether at a shop or a machine servicing centre.
It's a job which pays. You do not affect them.

But you ask only for acknowledgment to get help,
Orientation so you can find a direction pointing to help,
To find hope for some change in how you are.


## Sacred Oaths

Doctors used to be the only trainers of the martial arts
Because they knew how to heal and harm.
Now it seems they supervise torture
Because they know how to cause exquisite extreme pain.

Their healing light was partly their ability to cheer,
Balanced by knowing how to remove fear
But their art is changing into numbers needed to treat.

I count myself lucky or blessed or perhaps both
When my doctor smiles and asks me about my inner dialogue.
He is the only person interested in what goes on in me,
A man or a woman true to the sacred oath.

## Not Gobby

What a gossipy life this can be, but not in medicine,
As you can only anonymously tell stories to guide
But not amuse others.
Respect, compassion, trust, confidentiality
Make many doctors quiet, so they are not gobby.


## No More Work

No more work I said,
I don't have to work anymore.
But what I do now is work only on a different level.
On this other level
I now have to be to others what my elders were to me.
Just one more step, as always one more seems
To fuel the illusion that work will go sometime.
But work is only a word which before was just life.
How did we get to the illusion that ending it would be good?

## 16. WARRIORS

### Song for All Unknown Soldiers

I was only thirteen when they came to my school
I had no idea they were just looking for fools
I tried to see with wide open eyes
But what they wanted from me was heavily disguised.

The RAF, Army, Navy said they would pay
For all kinds of travel far far away
They promised me money, excitement and fun
All I had to do was simply carry a gun.

They could have had criminals, bullies or thugs
Not vulnerable children more interested in hugs
They promised us that they'd always be there
And what ever happened they'd really care.

When your last freedom's taken from you
That's when they tell you just what to do
I took orders but couldn't make requests
And my bullied mind never got any rest
Again and again, again and again.

Now when I think of what they got me to do
These people would force your children too
I was hit by a bullet that I couldn't see
It was memory of killing that impacted on me
Again and again, again and again.

Flashbacks by day, then nightmares in bed
I couldn't tell if they were real or just in my head
My innocence has gone but not the memories or pain
Of scenes of a war which was truly insane
Again and again, again and again.

On the crusade of the economy driven war
I soon realised these wars had all happened before
The deaths, the losses, keep on happening again
So the victories the medals are all just in vain
Again and again, again and again.

If you fight for peace war will happen again
Without negotiation and tolerance
It'll happen again, again and again.

Political bunkers protect leaders from war
While innocent children are blown to the core
They give the orders to kill everyone
But won't speak the truth to anyone
Again and again, again and again.

If you fight for peace war will happen again
Without negotiation and tolerance
It'll happen again, again and again.

Let girls just be girls and boys be boys
Let children be children and just give them toys
Stop our children standing on the front line
Use words not children now is the time
Again and again, again and again.

If you fight for peace war will happen again
Without negotiation and tolerance
It'll happen again, again and again.

The Crusades, Vietnam, the World and Gulf wars
Northern Ireland, Afghanistan what are we fighting for?
It's time now to stop blowing others a part
Not be frightened to listen to their heads and their hearts
Again and again, again and again.

## 17. TIME

### Illusions of What Is

Thoughts to fill in time, words to fill in time.
Speech to fill in time which cannot be filled.
If time doesn't exist, perhaps the Romans are beside us,
And our ancestors are beside us as well as inside us.

If time is nothing, then the illusion of it
May also make space an illusion of our condition.

Our condition may be temporary or permanent
But not neither, so in what do we exist?
Do we really exist just as we think we do
Or are we an illusion of the name and form of time and space?

### Penultimate

Turns out the final is only the penultimate
As there is almost always one more in us.

### Final Time

The final time, the final process,
The final draft, the final look the final book,
The final sigh, the final cries, the final night,
The final breath and then finally that look.

### Natural Ease

At the wrong time nothing can happen.
At the right time everything happens with natural ease.

## Time Zones

Working in different time zones
Is not working around the planet;
It is the planet working you,
The tail wagging the dog.


## Infants School

I thought there would be nothing there,
Maybe just a carpark
But there it was sixty years later,
The tiny playground,
The three foot white circles on the red brick wall,
We flicked cards at.
The gateway where my mother said goodbye.


## What Solitude Does

All this solitude what does it do?
I've learnt about what I am,
About how much other people mean to me.


## Some Days Are

Some days are just work, some days are just spiritual,
Some days are just family, some days are just history,
Some days are just forgetting, some days are just remembering,
Some days are just regretting, some days are just hoping,
Some days are just happiness, some days are just love,
Some days are just forgotten, some days are remembered,
Some days are just being, some days are just solitude,
Some days are just silent, some days are just still.

## Being There

My first abandonment was looking at my mother,
Waving at me.
She was leaving me at infant's school at five.
She waited for me to realise I was being left.
I gulped, sobbed tears and sucked in as if I was gasping for air.

I was drowning in the pain
Of being wrenched by being left there, of her leaving.
It was just for the day,
Not a term of months of painful abandonment,
Which all the borders felt,
When I moved school a couple of years later.

## No More Sitting Cross Legged

I was in denial until I realised no matter what,
I could no longer sit cross legged on the floor
And I had to sit on a chair at a table.

The hips, the back and knees couldn't take the strain
Without pain sitting where I had always sat,
Happily cross legged on the floor.

Denial for a week meant my feelings were being buffered
Whilst my body slowly let me know
This is what happens when you begin to grow old.

## Day and Night Person

I'm not a morning person, an evening person
Or any part of the day person.
Consciousness of being seems to comes and go,
Although it seems impossible to be aware all the time, we are.

## All Our Yesterdays

There are no new profound things to say or write
As they all seem to have been said and recorded,
And mostly ignored by almost everyone.
Perhaps there should be a ban
On trying to come up with new things.

Coming up with new things
Could be banned until the old is known,
Then the origin of any next step can be shown.
No new wars, second marriages
Until the previous one is known.

Active reflection on our history, our thoughts, actions,
Friendships, enemies, stories and all our yesterdays,
Could be shown and known.


## Final Day Every day

Always use your favourite bath salts.
Always wear your favourite shoes.
Always wear your favourite clothes.
Always wear your favourite aftershave or perfume.
Always say what's in your heart.
Don't ignore this, then reflect
And say I regret and wish I saw this, now, with little time left.
Write that letter, say that sentence,
Get that present for them or you.


## The Past

Nothing can change the past except I can accept it.
I can see it as a time of growth.
It was a necessary experience.

## The Final Phase

The surprises which you are told to expect
When you get old
Are just like the surprises which you are told to expect
When you are young.

The difference is, even though they are expected,
Then they arrive,
When you are old,
They are more of a shock than a surprise.

## Suddenly Apparent

Graveyards don't seem to have the same mystery
I remember as a child because just five years ago
The ground started to come up for me unexpectedly.
It was not at first noticed but then it shocked me
And only now graveyards have lost their mystery,

## More Years

Getting older doesn't make you stronger,
You've got a weaker body.
You've got more bad memories,
More traumatic events have accumulated.

The balance of losses and gains can't be assessed anymore
Because there are too many to make a noticeable difference.
The inevitable feels appropriate for the first time,
As what could be done was.
Who wishes for more years?

## Early September

It's always an awkward feeling this time of year.
Early September with the feeling of going
Back to the people at school, college or work,
After a break from the pressures of people in life.
I want my solitude back.
I want the happiness detached from the things of life.

Since childhood it's the same for most,
The end of happiness in early September,
Conditioned by education, family or work to end happiness.
I used to think one day it would come back,
But learnt it is only ever right here now
To be seized in these days of perfect peace.


## Sunday Night

Sunday night always has the feeling of all Sunday nights
Of something just about to end.
Neither here nor there,
There is the drawn out waiting for it all to end.


## Sunday after Three

Why is it only just Sundays, when the afternoon is fading,
That the tasks waiting for the next day
Always fill my heart with dread.

No other day or time brings this sense
Of wanting to avoid what we know has to be done.

Is it the familiarity of the routine, the automatic behaviour,
Instead of the freedom of walking away,
We know we would like to feel.

## Sunday in Two Minds Again

Sundays are part of my life
But have never been my favourite day.
Now, just as a child, it is the routine things that get to me.
They suddenly remind me the routine of another week is close.
Having a bath and getting things ready concretise it.

But where would I be without my Sundays?
There are memories of church as a child,
Sharing the bathwater,
Looking to the exciting good things the week could bring.

## Not of Time

Where does time go? It doesn't go anywhere.
It can't because it doesn't exist.
Time is a thought of measuring what doesn't exist.
Consciousness sees thoughts of time
But consciousness is not subject to time
As consciousness is not of time.

## The Journey Tells Us the Way

The Journey tells you the way.
There is no need to ask.
Just wait for it to speak back to you.

## Not Necessarily a Good Example

Would I show anyone else this way?
Maybe if they stayed around or came back asking,
Again knocking on my door, asking for more.

## The Dream

I want the dream to be over
To show me the truth of reality as it is.
Awake, sleeping or dreaming are all the same dream.
I know I know this which is the dream explained.


## Never both

You can be like everyone else
Or you can be yourself but never both.


## With Family

I was worried for a while, perplexed is more accurate
As I thought all along I was wrong until I found my search.
It seemed I ignored the material and looked odd,
Took all the wrong decisions.

Seemed like I was going to end up
With nothing.
All I am able to say is
This is as good as happiness gets.


## Obstructing Access

There is nothing wrong with man's body or brain
Only his thinking.
He has too little to do with his heart.
Consciousness of having a heart is overwhelmed by thoughts,
Eventually obstructing preventing access.

## Personal Vehicles

Sitting in a German car dealership
Waiting for a car's tyres to be replaced,
I sense our ever escalating wasteful use of resources
Should make us walk away forever from cars.

The car makers need us, we don't need them
As we could be healthier and wealthier walking.
The world would be less polluted.
We would speak more, sharing everything home grown.


## Heart's Servant

When thinking is not disciplined,
You either become overwhelmed by thinking,
Which seems to have a mind of its own,
Or you reject it and find an alternative.

You can go to the heart
And return there at every moment possible,
Leaving thinking only for its functions
As your hearts servant.

You can observe thinking and see its nature.
Thinking creates a cloudy picture of an ego
Which demands presence
When it does not even exist.

## 18. REFLECTION

### Note to Me

The last days,
I want to be more gentle however many there are.
I want to be more sensitive especially to me.

### One Final Path

There is no single formula which works best for turning inside
But whichever way we choose,
The final path is always the same.

### Knees

We rose from our knees over 70,000 years ago
And walked out of Africa probably talking then too
As we began to cover the earth like an infection.

When we walked, then talked,
Our thinking let us plan this journey
But the thinking brought us down.

The meteor which wiped out the dinosaurs
Was a pimple
Compared with the millions of times more damage
We have done since walking, talking and thinking.

It seems we can only wait for the final warnings
Of our extinction
Then we will be back on our knees,
On all fours.

## Being Here Now

We have been thinking like this since we walked out of Africa,
Thinking and dreaming we were going to arrive somewhere.
We have arrived at the dreams we dreamt,
But the dreams were not true.
Like our thoughts now seem real,
They were just our dreams in Africa.
What we were then did not threaten the survival
Of animals, plants or the planet,
But now we are the executioner the destroyer
Of everything we love.


## Wallowing

The commanders ensure there is no wallowing
In thoughts and feelings about lost friends
Even if you carried your best mate's coffin.
You must crack on immediately with the next task,
So that later, all you can do is pray.


## The Thread That Links Us

It is not how much time I have left,
It is what is going to be shown.
What will I experience, what will I uncover,
What is in store for me.
Who will I see, who will they be.
What have I got left to do, to be,
So I can leave what I see to you?
You may pick it up to look at some place along your path,
Then leave it to pass it on to someone else.

## Experiencing

Time to get rid of all the stuff I have acquired, given or bought.
Time to leave no things around, nothing behind.
Maybe just some words in the ether of the digital age,
Or even some words in a folder on a page.
Maybe only my experience not recorded anywhere,
Just experienced then over.


## Not Too late

I don't know how many days I have left
Or even if the next breath will come.
I'm not aware anything at all is wrong;
I'm just being clear and real about uncertainty.

I can't be thankful after the time has passed to be thankful.
I can't say what I mean
When the person can no longer hear me.

I only strive to be happy now in every one of my thoughts
In the words I say or write to show you.


## Two Types of Journey

Your body is under a death sentence.
Your mind takes less distress with age.
Traumatic memories accumulate with time.
Enthusiasm once peaked never returns.

The whole experience of life can seem to have a rotten end
Unless the desire for happiness
Transforms it
Into a thankful spiritual journey.

## Companions walk with us

Not in time but of time you see what you are.
There are no changes when the inside is seen.
Your heroines and heroes
Are mere companions walking with you.
We cannot yet see the oneness in our stillness.

## The Only Way

The only thing that brings you to the spirit
Is knowing the spirit is here.
Logic does not prove the spirit.
The only proof of spirit is the union of experiencing it.

The only thing that brings you to love is loving.
Logic does not prove love.
The only proof of love is the union of experiencing it.

## Not Still Enough to Move

I haven't been bent over by the wind
Or walked and been soaked in the rain much lately.
My sitting in stillness has been so disturbed,
I've not been able to be still enough
To actually move into stillness.

## Passing Something on

Most of our memories and reflections do not help,
But techniques of doing things
Are the best way to pass things on.

## Now I compare

When he came in the room you didn't seem to care.
Now his body is gone you see him everywhere.
You hated the sound of his old boots in your head,
Now you can't sleep if they are not by your bed.

The sound of him eating always put you in a mood,
Now you can't eat unless you hear yourself eating your food.
Funny how every sound is heard, every smile seen,
How we just glance as if this is how we will always be.

## Wonder

Wonder at the sky the moon and stars,
Wonder at the sun, wonder at the oceans.
Wonder at courage, wonder at humility,
Wonder at compassion. Wonder at consciousness,
Wonder at the sense of wondering is exquisite wonder.

## Eschatology

We do not live long enough
To see the changes in the shape of a river.
Even if we did, would we notice them?
We now live long enough
To see the repeating cycles of our own nature.
Even with this knowledge we do not change.

On the brink of catastrophe,
When annihilation is the alternative,
Does our thinking accept that it is incorrect?
There is a selfish greedy recklessness, competing until death
With effects on everyone,
Which even though some care about, can destroy us all.

## 19. OTHERS

### Making It Up

You couldn't make it up because it is life.
When you make it up, the lie loses the rawness of truth,
Just like you always know when an actor is acting.

### Usefulness

I accept that I am a worker for others
And whether I choose or not,
Someone will be profiting from me.
It is the same for us all.

### Leaders

The world gets the leaders it needs.
Their role is to restore the balance lost by those before them,
Whichever way.

### Just Being with One Person

Others amass more land, buildings, investments
And I wonder if their dreams are free.
Maybe they are more free because of these things.

My dreams seem to reflect
What I get deliberately get involved with.
They are not material things
But journeys, paths, spooky silent places.
Some are in other worlds.
Most are about being with one other person.

## Looking in Each Other's Eyes Again

Man's habit of making everything easier
By making them habits
Has led to everyone using things instead of themselves.
From not walking to not talking with no eye contact
And not playing to not physically taking part in life.

If man is brave enough to take some steps back,
We can learn to do, walk, talk, play,
Physically interact with the world
And look each other in the eye again.


## Gossip

Gossip is always full of energy
But the wrong kind to make anyone feel good
Because it is about other people.


## Stories

What we seem to others is the story we leave behind,
But the truth we live is what we are and is known only to us.


## One Exception

I can't keep up with this obsession with numbers.
One is the only one that is necessary.
One is all there is.
One being the exception
The rest are made up and an illusion.

## All Talk is Imagined

We don't have to imagine a conversation with anyone.
It happens before we say everything
Because we imagine their responses and ours to theirs.


## Differing Levels

Do you have to stay with those you don't like?
Do you have to work with those you don't like?
Do you have to eat with those you don't like
Or would you want to live off your own kind?


## One Two Three or More at My Door

Having to deal with just our self is a battle of duality.
Thoughts want to be uppermost in our mind as our ego,
But the peace of consciousness of being still was first.
This is our condition, which we accept or restore.

I don't flourish in groups.
I don't work in groups.
I am solitary
And prefer one to one company in all settings.

Listening to one person is complicated
As there are so many voices present who can't speak
Who influence what the person says,
So it is difficult to identify what the person wants.

Listening to a group is different.
They all speak not listening to each other,
Wanting to be heard as one voice
When they and can only be fragments.

## Renting

Renting something you own
Is renting part of you to someone else,
Whether a tool, a car, a house or even a body part like a uterus.
It never makes you feel better about yourself.


## All Mixed Up

When you meet someone,
It is not just a face with a body and a smile.
There is an unmeasurable amount of influence
Going back decades.

There are important ancient family histories,
Stories, legends and facts, scandals and gossip
Mixed with truth and beauty and the result is what you see.


## My wish

For today,
I wish to have time to be with the ones I choose,
To withdraw from the world,
To be thankful for being conscious
And for being happy.


## Thank You for Calling me Stupid

I am glad I was thought of then as being stupid,
Because otherwise now I could be seen
As not having got anywhere,
And still just being stupid.

## Playing Our Parts

What is said about what someone,
May have no relation to what they are like.
Better to leave what you think about them
As their work personality only.

What is said about what someone,
May have no relation to what they do for work.
Better to leave what you think about their work
As their work only.


## Our Small Talk

'So,' is the word to start every answer?
'You couldn't make it up,' is the current fashion
In complimenting someone's talking.

Underneath and unspoken,
The despair of emptiness is silenced
By the egos current fashion of ego's to satisfy each other.


## Of Our Kind

We all come from nobility.
It is just what we do with our inheritance that determines
If we are noble people or without dignity.

Treachery is always around
To raise the status of the other person,
But so is humility
To help us be accepted as of our own kind.

**Labels**

What we call someone sticks, like sticking a label on a jar.
What labelling doesn't change is in the jar.


**The Village Shop**

With all our knowledge, how come we don't use it intelligently
To spell out basics about ourselves
So that we can live more wisely?
More happily to see the real mechanisms
Behind how we relate?.
Why we take too many chemicals and food and drink?
How only a certain amount of work and wealth is good for us?
What different types of people we need and don't need?
How we can congregate together at times
And how we don't when we could
To improve our own and other people's lives?

The not for profit community shop
Staffed by volunteer's two hour shifts watch,
Protect and gather in the lonely,
The vulnerable who need little else.

## 20. REALITY

### Nothing to Do With Reality

Reality has nothing to do with thinking, psychology
Or religion.
Reality can only be seen if you are not distracted by thoughts.
Reality is everything else when thought is not present.


### Reality

Everything is as it appears to you.
It is exactly as it seems to you.
It is all there is and is a part of you.

All you actually have is you.
Reality is that there is just you.
Just you is all you can be, all you can know.


### Strange Discovery

The discipline of happiness comes only from suffering.
They exist only because of the each other.


### What Appears the Same

There are different ways to turn inside,
Suffering is the beginning,
Meditation and solitude are the middle;
Stillness is the same at the beginning, middle and end.

## Raw Energy of Stillness

When we step out of our shoes,
New ways lie ahead for those to walk in our shoes
With exactly the same energy we began with.

There is a raw energy which encourages nature and life
To simply be itself to the best it can be.
This energy waits inside us to show us what we are,
So we can show others too.

## Where to Find Truth

Only listen to the person who looks inside for truth.
It is the only place where you will find it.
Only listen to the person who looks inside for truth inside you.

## No Truth

If it's not you it's not Truth.
If it's not from inside you it's not truth.

## Finding Truth

Truth is not at school, college or university. It is in you.

## What You Can Only Learn One Way

You can't find out about yourself in books.
They can only confirm
What you found by turning inwards into yourself.

## Where Truth Is

You will finally see after much searching,
Sometimes after several decades,
The truth you look for, which you call reality,
Is only inside you.

## One Way, the Only Way

You find out about you from you.
Others can point the way.
Books can point the way.
Places can point the way but the way is turning inside.

## Inside Only

Just as you stay inside to keep warm in winter,
You can only find out about yourself by turning inwards.

## Love and Affection Always

Our love and affection is from the heart always.
Intangible affection, present always in everything,
Which is done or not done yet.
Our love and affection is here and there always.

## States of Being

This life is a dream between two states.
One is pre-birth the other is after-death.
We know nothing about either or even who or what we are.

## Still Good

The day's new born baby checks are done,
The expectant mothers are all seen,
The seventy three year old with terminal cancer has died
And the middle aged alcoholic is still in denial.
My room is a single cell where they all come and go,
Where I stay still, seeing I am having a good day.


## Most Full when Empty

I couldn't change to be concerned with only the material
As it would be like me cutting my leg off
Or being good at maths.
Why is this? What did this to me?
Was I born like this or did I become this?

I am most comfortable with no comforts.
I am full of happiness with nothing to want.
I am thankful for the worst things.
I feel most connected to everyone in solitude.


## Seems Like Reality

The world we experience is only what we choose
But we are usually unaware that we choose.
We then interpret our experiences so seek meaning,
Unaware we are only questioning our own choice.
When we see the world is our creation
Interpreting it and trying to find meaning stops.
It is not what it seems like at all it is only our interpretation.

## Who is The Doer

At the end of struggling we have to give up control
To whatever is our inner self, as it has us in its jaws.
Whatever we do, it is not us who does it.
It is the one who has us inside who does it,
Who is none other than our own self.

## True to Our Own Self

If what we believe to be true is what our mind tells us,
Because it has integrated all inputs from our senses
And rationalised an answer as a conclusion,
Then everyone's truth is different.

Everyone's truth being different because it is relative
Means there is only our own truth.
We can only be loyal to that one truth, our truth,
Which is being true to our self.

## Consciousness as a Temporary Resident

Maybe consciousness is not actually inside us
And is not centred anywhere in space.

Perhaps it is something everywhere we can connect to
Or not depending on the strength of our signal.

## Thought

I am not sure what to think or how to think,
Why to think any more when experience is so much better.
We overuse this lofty apparatus,
Missing out on much that would make us happy.

## Confirmation of Truth

Although we think we know, we do know.
When we see we are not the body at all
But just using it for this journey,
It is confirmation of what we are is truth.

What this truth is,
Seems to be the stillness within,
Which if patiently sought and stayed with,
Is seen to be in everyone in everything.


## Not a Clue

We haven't got a clue about what we are doing
As we only see when it is nearly over and too late,
Which applies to almost everything.


## We Know

We are fortunate to be born and we don't know why.
We are born into happiness and suffering
And we don't know why.

It is an incredible experience and we don't know why.
It is full of beauty and ugliness and we don't know why.

We are conscious and we don't know why.
We die with happiness and sadness and we don't know why.

## Say it Can

When you are the only person who can do it,
If you say it can't be done, you add to the likelihood
That it can't be done.
So just say it can.

## The Same Unique Difference

I have gone off on a tangent on a path.
I thought it was just me but when I asked,
It seems like I'm not the only one.
We are so uniquely different that we are the same
Because each of us has so many differences.

## Even Wrong is Right

What a colossal relief to know the path I took was right,
That the people I have been following were right,
That where I am now is right.
It could not be otherwise. How could it be?
Even wrong is right as it is seen to change.

## Breaking Attachment

There is nothing more painful
Than seeing the one you love suffer at the hands of others.
There is nothing more worrying
Than fearing what will happen to them.
Letting go of them is impossible
But necessary for you both to survive.

## Finally

Finally we don't see with light, we see with inner light.
Finally we don't hear sound, we hear with inner silence.
Finally we are not aware with the mind,
We are aware with inner stillness.


## Freedom as a Chain

When you have detached, it is difficult to attach again
Because there is no reason or desire,
As false freedom has been let go of.


## What we Are

Truth cannot be argued with,
Only seen for what it is,
Acknowledged for what it is,
Then accepted for what it is.


## About You

Enough of this from me because this is now about you,
How you see it.
It may take years to see this,
Even if it takes decades, it is all about you,
Which is what you need to pass on.

## As Close to Truth

Is it possible to separate reality from our thinking?
What we think cannot be reality for everyone.
What we interpret as reality is usually only our perspective
From our thoughts.
But if we stop thoughts and stay with what is here,
We see being conscious of existence is as close as we can be.


## Thinking and Reality

It is so difficult to see what is going on now
Because we are so busy doing things, thinking things.
It is so difficult to see where we are now
From the distance of the future because that vision is blind.

The ability to see perfectly is always here but obstructed
By what we are thinking and doing,
We usually only see what we are thinking or doing,
Not what we are.

What we are is obscured by thinking.
Thinking is a thick fog stopping us from seeing reality.
If we could see this, it could scare us so much
We might get in denial about it
Because we couldn't deal with it.

## Most Powerful Desire of No Thought

So you now know you cannot trust anyone else
And you have to trust yourself.
But be just as careful not trusting your body,
Even though you look after it and nurture it in every way
Because it can suddenly fail you
With cancer and other fatal diseases.
So you are left with only trusting yourself.

Then you discover that thoughts won't stop
And they keep you awake at night.
Thoughts keep you worrying about the future,
Stopping you being happy now.
How do you slow, them stop them, and abandon them?

Slowing and stopping them can last
For a few seconds or minutes.
This is by tethering them by concentration one thing.
But they return trying to get some shape in the form of the ego.
Being identified as an entity called the ego
Gives them a reason to keep on forming.
Mercifully, the ego can only be stopped by seeing this.

For this to happen
You have to give up wanting any thoughts ever again.
Not wanting any thoughts is above all else.
This means your ego has to go.
Complete surrender is a possible alternative.
Do you really want this?

## 21. LIFE FROM OUTER SPACE

### Would They be like Us

Would Martians have cats and dogs as pets
And friends for company and exercise?
Would they have stuffy establishments
To show they could endure financial wastage?
Would they gamble and eat out rather than in,
Sleep so much, eat and drink so much?
Would Martians be more like insects
And thin rather than obese like us?

### Leave Us

When man discovers there is life on other planets
And eventually visits to see
If there is any chance of a relationship,
Could this be the result?

'We do not want you to stay so please leave us now.
We only want to be with intelligent life forms
Who respect others and their ways of life?'

### The Visit

The visitor looked at us and said,
'What you do to your weather, killing each other,
Eating your friendly faced friends?

No time for stillness, solitude, silence, spirit nurturing.
Drinking that false spirit, taking those chemicals
Because you can't control your mind on your own,
I'm going home.'

## 22. SELF NURTURING

### Realignment

Sometimes you have to step to the side
To get out of someone's way.
Sometimes you have to get out of the light
To let the light shine on someone.

When you need re-aligning get out of your own way.
Get out of your light so your inner self can just be.

### Stand in Your Way or Understand

Get over yourself and begin to see what is behind your ego.
We are all given the same by nature,
But we choose what we become and want to stay as.
Either get out of our own way or stand in your own way.

### Just be

Empty blank surface we are obsessed with changing you.
Just as it is difficult to leave you alone,
So we struggle to just be our self without thoughts.

### Our Own Heart

We are just workers, our concerns not seen,
Our personal caring touch not valued because it has no price.

Perhaps our continued personal touch,
Kept secret from the powers that seem to rule,
Lets us rule our own hearts.

## Un-mysterious Stillness

Thinking and religions want mystery.
The Self wants the stillness of truth.

## Un-mysterious

We become lost in the wanderings of the mind
Because the nature of the mind is inquisitiveness,
To keep moving.
The mind loves mystery because it loves to solve.

Mystery solving gives it its identity and reasons to survive.
When there are no mysteries,
The mind begins to settle in simplicity and ignore complexities.
Then serenity can settle like snow on dry land in stillness.

## Mysteriousness

Don't be fooled by the mysterious.
The mysterious is what they say you haven't got
Because it's just bait.
A mysterious man and a mysterious truth
Are contradictions in terms which fool our mind.

We prefer the mysterious future rather than the plain present.
Our minds prefer complications rather than simplicity.

Religions thrive on us being drawn to mystery,
The only mysterious thing is our ignorance
Of preferring mystery instead of truth.

## So We May Be together

Yes I feel odd, a stranger in my own country
Detached from the things of life.
Like a squirrel prefers to gather nuts,
I prefer to work on my own.

Yes there will be a time when the fruit is shared.
Until then and after I will return to my gathering,
Getting things together, so we may be together.


## Humility and Compassion

If you are powerful, famous and rich
And don't have humility and compassion
You can never be happy and happy for others.

If you are poor
And only have humility and compassion
You are happy for yourself and for others.


## Goodness Never Hides

People hide away when they know
You have seen what they are like,
Unless they have goodness in their hearts
Which you would never hide away.


## A Visit

Sometimes, someone dropping in changes your perspective.
Maybe it's their song that picks you up,
Out from your engrossed thoughts.

**Let the Good In**

Good people are the only ones we should let into our life.
Keep the others out as much as you can.

It is impossible to do this forever
But the process must be maintained.
Then the will is passed on and repeated time and again.


**Difficult to See**

Occasionally, only when another person comes across someone
You thought you knew, you find out what the person thinks.

It is not deceit or dishonesty at work
But that we can project so much onto someone,
That we seldom see them for real.


**Subtraction not Addition**

No one sees in darkness but that's what we try and achieve,
To remove the darkness, so we can see clearly what is there.

It applies mostly to our inner self
To try and understand what it there
But the darkness only has to be removed.
Nothing needs to be added.

This is what can't be understood, that nothing new is needed.
Removing what is not needed is a subtraction not an addition.

## Principles

Time after time we return to the same few principles.
There are few which keep us on track on our path.
Simplicity, humility and compassion.

## 23. SMILE

### Smile

A smile can change your whole day,
More than words in a book,
More than a week off.

### Most Memorable Today

At least I made someone smile today:
A five year old girl and a four year old boy,
A woman with no money to pay for her pills
And a man with not enough patience.

### A Smiling Life

As a boy I wanted to be spiritual,
But not a priest performing rituals or giving blessings.
I wanted the peace of a place
Where there was no fighting for peace,
Just peace.

I didn't want to be anything.
I just wanted to be me happy
With the serenity of the peace I saw in Franciscan monks.
I wanted to do something
Which would bring a smile to others and me.

Decades have passed.
The boy is the same and I now know what I did.
I just smiled at people when we saw each other.
Maybe it was easier than praying.

**The Joy of Joy**

I had enough after a short spell
Acting being an elder of the tribe,
Making seemingly important statements.
I quickly reverted to my younger silent self,
Watching for twinkles in the eyes, smiles.
What joy there is in joy.


**The End of Stories**

The hospital discharge summary, which is how it works,
Was just bullet points: -

-Age 76
-Address Single room apartment
-Transport Walking
-Problems Frailty, Arthritis, Depression, High blood pressure.

It missed: -

-War veteran with shrapnel in legs.
-Widowed.
-Dependants, looks after his disabled daughter,
 A dog and a cat.
-Looks after the neighbour's unemployed son.
-Anxiety about his untended vegetables in his allotment.

A man, who walked miles out in the cold
To put flowers on his wife's grave,
Then shared them with others.

He is quiet and helps patients get through their ordeals.
He didn't mention the friends he lost.
He always gives you his smile for free.

## Be What You Are

Whether or not we admit it, we all live by a set of rules.
To live well and be happy we need to ask
If these are our own rules,
Or are they someone else's rules.

I write my own rules down, check them
And reflect to see if I still feel OK about them,
Or if they need adjusting.
Writing them down makes you clearer about you.
Cringe-worthy though they may seem, here are my own rules.

To be happy, spend as much time as you can being still,
As it will keep you on the path you are on.
Call it anything, meditation, special time,
And realise it is always with you.
Be a weirdo, be odd, be abnormal, don't fit in, fit out.

Be yourself, kind with compassion.
Keep everything simple and smile at yourself.
My rules sometimes work for me.
Everyone else's sometimes work for them.

Be firm and flexible and aim for happiness.
Don't waste time
Wanting to get to some stage of your life faster
As some things can't be controlled,
Especially when you are old.

Eat fewer root vegetables because they concentrate chemicals.
Eat just enough. Eat more fruit, nothing processed.
Walk slowly, ride and drive slowly,
Think slowly and smile when you can.

Go barefoot or have good shoes,
And don't forget to sleep in the open as well as in a good bed.
You spend most time in both.
Spend as much time outside as possible but don't sunbathe.
Walking is the best exercise.

But don't do anything dangerous unless you have to.
If you do, don't do it without crash landing gear.
And when it is over smile.
Don't see sad films, read sad books or listen to sad music.
Treat others with the manners
A servant would show to a King or Queen,
Then everyone is respected.

Only see good friends, don't use them or pay them.
Stick with positive people not negative people
And return other people's smiles.
Be as wrong as right but don't take daily matters into the night.
And give your smile whenever there is a chance.

Thinking is not your master only your friend.
Your master is not your ego which you see as yourself
But instead it is your inner self.
Happiness is the single aim of your life. Show your smile.

**What is Your Perfect Day?**

Rain everywhere, windscreen wipers going
With grey skies but fantastic views over the Severn Bridge.
A perfect day, with my daughter who is at a party later.
I see old friends later too but she's staying overnight,
To sleep tight to awake and smile at another perfect day.


**Infectious**

How good it is to be positive, to celebrate the positive,
To seek out the positive and to smile with it
Whenever the opportunity appears.

How infectious it is to smile at someone else.
They always reflect back how they are,
Sometimes giving back the gift
Of an unexpected beautiful smile,
Or just that they want to smile.


**That Smile**

We really are such a complex mess,
Not as straightforward as we would like,
Each carrying our ancestor's history around like a heavy load.
Our history may be seriously heavy.

Understanding it can be a long task
And until it is worked through we hide behind a mask.
No one is free of this as our past is inescapable like our fate
And this is why, maybe we should smile more.

# OUR RESPONSE TO THE WORLD

## 24. FEAR

### Thinking and Breathing Fear Away

Thinking starts fear and we then lose control of our breathing.
But we can use our thinking
To slowly get back control our breathing.
Breathing is not only a barometer of fear
But breath control is the best extinguisher of fear.

### Fear of the Unreal

Sequential, logical thinking creates the concept of time
By recalling memories and imagining the future.
Thinking shows the past and future to be concepts,
As our past and future are our thoughts.

Our whole life can be spent fighting against time
Whose inevitable consequences we try to avoid.
It is better to have a still mind.

### Propulsion

Fear is behind all our worst behaviours
And our dream is a day without it.
How can what appears to motivate us
Seem to be our worst enemy?

It keeps us alert and alive being aware of the consequences.
Fear is a propellant into the future not staying in the present.
Its enemy is the present. With a still mind fear is left behind.

## Spreadsheet of fear

We don't know the day we will die.
The date and time are all we can't be told yet.

The worry would begin the day of the news an announcement,
Like an explosion changing all our moments ,
From cherished ones to hopeless ones.

If we knew, how many could cope or would care more?
A new kind of fear with a date
Could appear instead of the old known fear.

Scientists haven't got the information to become our life's
Accountant with a spreadsheet of fear of our life and death.
Let's hope and try to ensure they never do.


## Being in Control

We keep old ways of thinking, thinking we can stay in control.
We keep our old fears, thinking we can control our fear.

Old ways are chosen as the best
Because they are easy and comfortable
But comfort to avoid change can blind us to what has changed.

We blame everything to avoid admitting
We are not really in control and something else is.

We need to own up, give up the thinking that holds us back
And give control back to whatever is in control.

A little less holding on, a little less control,
A little less blame and we can let go.

## Fear

Fear stops now from being felt.
It blocks consciousness.
It is our best friend and worst enemy.
But we don't seem to be able to live without it.

Fear is a response demanding attention
As you can't just be when it is present.
Fear is a prison made of the mind and it is not often kind.
Fear takes your breath, it takes your body.
It takes higher consciousness down to basic reactions
Of fight of flight then loss of consciousness.

Fear blocks and stops smiling and living.
It raises a wall to keep it in.
It is an isolating draining form of strain.
Fear can steer everything for all of our life
Or it can be seen and left alone with one single good breath.


## Fear as Your Friend

Stop trying to be so reasonable and instead be unreasonable.
Be absolutely certain about uncertainty.
Look at what you are not looking for.
Let fear of not being happy lead you.

Plug yourself into an energy supply of positive people.
You will burn brighter and shine with their energy.
They will help you turn fear into fuel
And live off the dread of panic,
Until even though you search it out, fear cannot be found.

## Endlessness

Endless images inside, pressures to comply to provide outside.
Pressures to conform, to obey rules not to be broken
And not allowed to be a fool.
Fear of failing, fear of fear, fear of sadness.
I'll stick with myself and my happy madness.


## Your Worst Fear

Let your worst fear happen to you in your mind.
Imagine you fall over and that everyone sees your underwear.
Let it happen several times
And you will be laughing at what used to be your biggest fear.


## Psychological Jail

Letting go of regrets,
Letting go of fear releases us into the present.


## Letting go of Fear

Fear is the worst thing to carry around.
Unpredictable it steals our happiness.
Fear of not liking ourselves, fear of not being liked,
Fear of not being approved, fear of abandonment.
Fear can be let go of like throwing a stone into a pond,
Don't hold on to the stone as you throw it,
Just let it go its own way.
Do you think about where that stone landed
After you threw it skimming the water?
Don't give thought to fear
And fear won't give you thoughts.

## Turning negative to Positive

Turning fear to fuel is not an easy change from avoiding it,
But if you try and do what makes you scared,
You might get better about what is scaring you.

So much so, you can't wait to feel fear
And do what you are scared of,
Because you know performing comes next.
Then you see that the bigger the fear,
The better the performance.

## Calm Panic

Panic is a groove easy to fall into
And a little more difficult to get out of because you get stuck.
A gentle self reminder repeated endlessly
To breathe slow until the message is home restores calm.

## Confrontation for Progress

Fear of hesitating, fear of failing, fear of being overwhelmed.
Avoiding fear of these ensures fear will get worse.
If you don't deal with confrontation,
It can deal with you without mercy.
If you don't seize the opportunity to confront something,
It is turned into a loss.
If you give it a go, whatever the result,
It can be built on next time, which is progress.

## No Surprises

Knowing yourself brings an honesty to all actions,
With no fear of surprises.

## Normalising

Soldiers don't forget the fear that kept them alive.
Sometimes it was right
But not now in the middle of the night.

Letting go of conditioned fear is strange.
Letting go of being afraid is new.
Letting go of what might happen,
Takes practice and conditioning too.

Not being afraid in a safe place is normal
But can take a lot of practice to feel normal,
Then be normal.


## Letting Go of Approval

We are programmed and conditioned
To want to be thought of highly by those above and below us,
But needing approval can give control of us over to them.

Putting and leaving our self-esteem in other's hands
Is asking and waiting for trouble
Because disapproval is inevitable.
Approval of what we are is only ours.


## Don't Stick with Fear

By sticking with fear it sticks with you.
If you move away just a little,
Turning around,
Distracted, it loses its grip and power.

## Overwhelmed

Being overwhelmed by fear, pain, loss, depression,
Someone else, having no hope
Are all eclipsed by understanding.

What is it trying to teach us? What can we gain?
What is it showing us, where our happiness is?

How do you cover yourself
And sneak out dry from under a rainstorm?
There is a way out to find. You have to find it in your mind.


## Like Passing Clouds

Thoughts and feelings come then they go.
They are not forever. They are replaced by others.

If we dislike a thought or feeling. If it produces fear or loathing,
We can let it go, then think or feel a different one.

Thoughts and feelings are not compulsory.
They persist or are freed by our choice and need.


## Today is Now

So the day has arrived, inner stillness has replaced fear.
The time was here all along.

All it was trying to achieve was the calmness of being still,
Stopping thinking taking over.

## Encouraged To Be Fearful

Why is it fear is around all the time and happiness isn't?
Is fear more valuable to our survival,
Even if it means we are unhappy?

Is fear programmed in us from toddlers?
If happiness is our nature,
Then why are we encouraged to be fearful
Not happy most of the time?
Why are we encouraged to be fearful, not our true self?

If past results show that we only get hurt some of the time,
It is better to be happy most of the time
Than being fearful most of the time.
Maybe we could try.

## Primal Fear

Fear freezes us more than anything, even more than cold itself.
Fear paralyses us so we can't do anything,
As if we are numbed into inactivity.

Fear is such a primitive warning of things to come;
We can never ignore fear unless it is the fear when we know
Nothing is going to happen,
When we know it is imagined by us.

This fear we imagine, feels as real as the fear
Before something which is going to happen
But when we know it won't, it wastes a lot of our life.

## Above All Else in Life

When you have been through the shock
Of seeing a person you know taken,
Like a candle put out by the wind,
Then you have seen what life is like.

This does not go away
But is an introduction to the events on their way,
Some generous giving joy and warmth,
Others threatening to take your life away.

This is when we turn inwards
To what we know and trust the most
Because above all else in life,
It does not let us down, as it is us.


## Happiness, Fear and Thinking

Fear is why we don't do most of the things we could
Or we should.
Thinking the right way is why we would do these things
If only thinking could just stop producing fear.


## Why We Should Look Up

We need to look up when we are walking
To see where we are going in life.
To check the ground is safe enough
To see we are heading in the right direction.

We need to look up to say, 'Hello in there'
To the homeless, to strangers, to children, to old people,
To say hello to everyone, like and not alike us.
Try it for five minutes one day once in your life.

## Why We Look Down

Why do so many look down when they are walking?
I can understand if its uneven ground,
Cracked or uneven pavements,
And especially if it is because of dog or horse shit.
But many of us look down when we are walking
Out of fear in case when we look up someone will mug us.

In America they teach you to tell your burglar or mugger,
'I haven't seen you so I can't identify you.'
They say it is less likely they will shoot you with a gun,
But this lets burglars and criminals win
And is how the world changes in their favour
And perpetuates fear.
Perhaps if we looked them in the eye they might change.


## Dissolving Fear with Stillness

You speak about the fear you saw,
Fear you are scared of having again,
How it ripped out all the joyful moments
Of those precious days as a child.
You run like an athlete to avoid it,
But by running and avoiding
You never stop to look inside at stillness
And this is what can dissolve your fear.


## Why We Do and Don't

Fear is why we don't do most of the things we could or should.
Happiness is why we do everything.

## Happiness and Fear

Fear is experienced when you don't want it
But conjure it up by thinking.
Happiness can't be experienced when it is here all the time
And we desire it.

Fear is why we don't do most of the things we could
Or should do.
Thinking with all its reasoning
Doesn't seem to stop fear or help us be happy.


## Treachery

Even though most people are good
There is always a wolf amongst the sheep.
But the most dangerous situation
Is when there is a sheep amongst the wolves.
So there is deception, manipulation playing games
Until everyone is fooled that everyone is the same,
Then everyone is betrayed by treachery.

## 25. DOUBT

### Doubts

It is our nature to have doubts.
Their effect is like friends who never stop reassuring us
That we are serious about what we have chosen.

### Doubtless

As night is understood and fades into dawn
Because just as the world turns,
So doubt melts when confronted.

### Normal is Difficult

Why can't I be normal like everyone else
But I am told I am normal?
Well if this is normal then it is pretty difficult being normal.

Normal is what I would call
Being subject to what happens outside me,
As well as to what happens in others
And also to what happens in me.

Worse is what I just sit here and imagine,
Fearful about the future with no place now to rest
From this fearful, over thinking restless mind.
Yes this is normal.

## Double Doubts

How come doubts don't get weaker
And why do they seem stronger with the passing of years?
Then I realised it is because my stronger certainty
Needs stronger doubt to counterbalance it.

Doubt is one of our strongest friends.
Doubt arrives to check we are doing the right thing,
Then to reassure us that we are.
It makes us stronger, more confident and more grounded.
Doubt balances certainty.

Welcome the fear which doubt brings
Because it is only your inner self trying to alert to you.
Treating doubt with the hospitality
We would give our most trusted friend,
Lets doubt show us its message.
Welcome doubt without fear
And ask it what it has to teach you.

Thank doubt that doubt appears
Because it makes us more conscious
And lets us know we are normal.
You will be more confident if you make a good friend of doubt.
Like having friends, it is our nature to have doubts.
They never stop reassuring us we are serious.

## 26. ATTITUDE

### Change the Tyre

A bad attitude is like a flat tyre,
You can't go anywhere until it is changed.
It is not anyone else but you who needs to change.

Your attitude is your choice belonging to no one else.
Your attitude may be your last freedom
Or even your last words.

You can lose everything but not your attitude.
You can only change it,
So it is up to you how you want your final mood.

How you want to feel, what you want to say,
What you choose to think,
Remember it is your attitude, your personal way.

### Attitudes

What are my attitudes?
Where did I get them?
Do any need to change or be altered?
Do they stop me being happy?

My attitudes are how do I look at certain
People, activities, places and things I can be?
How do they affect others
And what do they do to me?

Do any need creating, adopting,
Cropping or dropping?
If they do, I change too.

## Respectful

I try to work out how to make a day positive
Whatever circumstances I find myself in
Because I know that my attitude influences the outcome.

I repeatedly realign my attitude and say to myself,
'I will be polite to everyone.
My manners will be as good as I can make them.

When I am helping someone,
I will be kind and I will be thankful
That I am not the person I am trying to help.'


## Being Within

Seeing what the inner world of our own self is like
Changes out attitude to the outer world.
We become thankful that our inner happiness
Can change our attitude to everything.


## Forgiving Our Self

Are we ever forgiven for what we have done?
Do we ever forgive us?
Can we change our attitude to what we did and why
And wish us well that we learnt from it?
Our attitude can change anything we want to.


## Shifting an Attitude

Not being thankful is a lesson not yet learnt
Because our attitude is frozen.
When our attitude moves, thankfulness is felt.

## Attitude

A happy heart carrying the weight of life.
A happy song sung with a lightness of heart.
A positive outlook about everything,
Especially as most things are not luck but choices.


## When You Look Back

In your last days what will your conclusion be?
Did you not care?
Was everything about you?
Was it just about fun?


## Did you have no principles?

Did you have a purpose?
Who were you?
Did you contribute to others?
Were you kind?
Did you help?
Were you decent?


## Instead of Revenge Imagine

Your display of power and assault
Were aimed to maim me,
To cause pain and destroy me.

Instead the tenderness you could not destroy
I want to give to you.
I want my tenderness to help you realise
You cannot imagine further assault on anyone.

## Waiting for Tears

Why can some people cry so easy and I can't?
What stops my tears?

Is it denial because I am not ready yet?
Fear of what would pump them out and down my face?

Blocked, stuck, not ready, fear, not enough support,
No answer to them.
Just being with my tears is what I want.

Just being able to be with my tears is what I wait for.


## Mistaken Moments

There are moments when everything seems
Coloured with dark doom, but they are only moments.

There are moments when thinking makes us believe
Nothing will be ok, but it is not all the time.

There are moments when we cannot see
The worth in anything, even us, but only for a while.

There are moments when we cannot see light,
When we think too much,

But these are moments when we only see our ego,
Not our happy inner self which is always there.

## Our Duty

Oceans are sometimes calm, sometimes rough,
Just as we too are an ever changing mix.
Our attitude can be balanced or not and may need adjusting,
So peaceful balance between opposites
Can be restored again as a lifelong duty.

## 27. NORMALLY ABNORMAL

### Endless Types of Personality Types

Personality disorders are regarded as abnormal
But may cause no trouble to others.
Psychiatric disorders are regarded as abnormal
But may cause no trouble to others.
Personality types are regarded as normal
But can be big trouble to others.
They are all words to describe us
When they are only words not us.
They are the map, not the actual territory.

### Only Two Races of People

The Second World War settled
The different types of people forever.
Viktor Frankl an inmate of Auschwitz frequently said
That there are only two races of people,
The "race" of the decent man
And the "race" of the indecent man.

### The Same Once in the Crowd

People sit in different places, postures,
With different intentions, moods, problems,
With different histories and different genes
But we are basically the same.

### No Wants

Not wanting anything is the best barometer of happiness.

## Our Influence

Everything is as it is meant to be.
If we change it, it is because it was meant to be changed,
So perhaps we only imagine our influence.


## Alright

I have difficulty not assessing things personally,
Because that is how I see the world
And this is what I have become,
From how I have experienced things.

I can't see things so impersonally, objectively
Like an informed judge.
I'm a bit more jumbled up by life and sometimes,
I don't come out perfectly right.

I'm alright but I'm not always alright.
I wasn't made perfectly
But that too is alright.


## Standing Back

Can you stand back not judging?
Can you be quiet when you could speak?
Can you just let things be?
Could this sometimes be me?


## Great Peace

In days of great peace, nothing happens.
In the stillness of days of great peace,
There is just the peace of stillness.

## What Turns Us Inside?

For all our logical thinking.
For all our verbal processing and reasoning.
For all our knowledge and technology,
The absence of thought shows us our inner self.

## Conscious Integration

Can you have different attitudes at the same time?
Can you hold more than one view
Seeing things more than one way?
Can you be objective and personal
As well as be clear and imaginative?
Can you read everything just visually
And see everything in terms of words?
Can you hear with your vision and listen with your eyes?
Can you integrate different attitudes,
Perceptions and judgements?
Can you be conscious of them all, then that too,
With compassion?

## If the World is Conscious

If everything is our best guess,
Then the world we think we see
Must be laughing at our thinking.

## Anything Could be Real

There is no agreement about psychology about religion,
The origins of the universe about physics or archaeology.
We don't know what is normal.
All perceptions and judgements are only our best guess.

## Abandoning Abandonment

Giving up all attempts to be normal
Is freedom from other people's rules.
Giving up norms is finding our own normality
Which is what we value above all else.


## Effortlessness

When the struggle is finished, like a dark distant storm,
We know there is only temporary effortlessness.


## Happiness is Inside

Those who tell you how happy they are,
And tell you all the things you can have to be happy too,
Are not usually happy.


## The Longest Book

In the quietest stillness
More can be processed and communicated
Than from the longest book.


## Isn't It Strange How

Only through solitude you learn how to be with others.
Only through silence you learn how to communicate.
Only through stillness you learn how to move.
Only through being you know.

## 28. IMPORTANCE OF BEING WEIRD

### Wiser

Next time you look at someone and see them as a fool,
Question how superior your thinking judgement is.
Has the fool seen how thinking can be our greatest enemy
And chosen to watch the stars instead.

Next time you look at someone and see them as a fool,
Ask why are they smiling and you are not.
Ask why they are happy and you are not,
Then consider if they have chosen wisely and you not.

### Eerie

Do you get a sense of eeriness more than others?
Does it make you feel connected in ways we can't describe?

Does the sense of eeriness around you
Stay when you think it has gone?
Is it with you at night when you sleep?

I thought it was just me but almost everyone seems to get this.
Everyone I've asked thinks they would seem abnormal,
So they never mention it.
Perhaps being more open about it would normalise eeriness.

### Brief Meeting

Unknown to you at first,
A brief meeting with your inner self
Can lead to the point of your life.

## The Ones at the Back

Some people always seem to be standing back,
Not at the front, not eager to engage but watch from a distance.

They don't expend armies of energy
Participating in events of the world.
They just run their own life of enjoying the present moment.

They are watchful, always seeming stationary,
Waiting for change, even though they don't move.


## Strange One

Do you often feel as if things are a bit vague,
That you are in a strange state, different from others?

Do you feel as if you are different,
Moulded in different ways, in ways you cannot say?

Join me in being weird
But happy in what we are.


## One Offs

When some bulbs we plant are different and do not flower,
When some trees are different and do not bear fruit,
Do we blame the sun?

When someone lets us down,
When we behave badly,
Who should we not blame?

**My Fantasy World**

I can't watch drama on television, I can't watch most plays.
I can't read complicated involved novels,
Because what people don't match up to
Are what I see every day.

Reading, theatre, television
Remind me of my job,
So forgive me if the way I relax is to stay in a world of fantasy.

**Weirdo**

Whoever said it was not good to be weird
Doesn't know it is good to feel weird,
To think weird, to see weird, to be weird.

**Challenges**

Some days I know I'm not doing enough for myself
To just be me.
I don't take enough chances with people.
Yet walking by the river, just for me,
I have to see what that shiny object on the ground is.
I have to reach that far off gate and touch it
Before I turn around, not tomorrow, now.

**Making Your Wish Come True**

Identify and concentrate on your wish.
Say what you want and how you want it
Assertively to yourself,
Then simply to others too.
Only then is your wish possible.

## Normally Abnormal

What if this path doesn't go home
But leads to other places including happiness, suffering
And then dying alone?

Accepting what are not normal outcomes are what we are,
Open, not seeking, just being still
With adventures warming the heart.


## Winking Dark Clouds

The past was shadowed like a dark cloud
Following me everywhere,
Darkening what could have been brighter moods,
Until I decided to use it.

I decided to look at it, to write about it then to sing inside me.
'It's going to get brighter. I'm gonna fight ya with happiness.
I'm gonna fight ya with light.'

The Dark cloud now winks at me from a distance
As it looks around for other victims.
Perhaps it's just the singing.


## Wondering

Wonder can be a blessing and a curse.
To wonder about the stars can open the soul or stop the mind.
Wondering about wonder is both.

## Inner Peace

Inner peace is a blessing melting away the negative,
The positive outlook reinforced.
Anxious vigilance depletes efforts to be positive in outlook.

## Inner Beauty

It is not the beauty in the light of a sunset,
In the contours of the mountains or in the rivers of the earth
But in us where beauty is.
Beauty is inside, behind the eye expressed with a smile
And always inside.
Shared beauty takes us further inside to the light.

## Divine Inspiration

Divine inspiration is supposed to be regarded as the only thing
That logic cannot challenge or argue with.
If you write from the heart of yourself
And if you are an Advaitan,
Then your self is god, so your writing is divinely inspired.

In Christianity where the Kingdom of heaven
Is said to be within,
Then god is inside you, so if you write from your heart
It could be divinely inspired.

I haven't got as far as looking at other religions
Because it seems if you can see it is true for one
And you understand it is true,
Then the truth the divine is you.

## Seeing and Listening

I value by sight but not above all else, not above consciousness.
Sight is not consciousness, nor is hearing or doing.
Consciousness is life.


## Not Much to Ask

My own rules are, spend time being still every day,
Which should keep me on the path I am on.

Keep things simple.
Treat others with the manners
A king would expect from a servant,
Then everyone is respected.

Be as wrong as right but don't take daily matters into the night
And leave happiness whenever there is a chance.


## Redundant Thoughts

Perhaps I have let my thoughts run riot writing
And now they need to be reeled in so it stops.
It has produced little of importance,
Except perhaps confirmation it is redundant.


## Now and Then

People I knew thirty years ago who knew me then
Would not know me now and I would not know them.
Why is this? We know each other as well as we did then.
It is just we are doing other things which we don't know about.

## Odd One Out

Being the odd one out, you eventually see
There are a lot of odd ones out, lots of us.
So many that the only conclusion is
The ones who are not odd are the odd ones.
We are the sane ones because we are so crazy about life,
Crazy about love.
It is for being and living, not thinking about.


## Anti-establishment Establishment

I started off being regarded as sensible by the establishment,
Then I refused to agree to conditions of living,
Which to me were like killing myself,
So I walked and walked until I was far away.

One day I was surprised when someone told me
I was the establishment.
Shocked, I asked how did this happen?
I had walked so far away from the establishment that
I could see without all the attachments, because I was detached.


## Things Other Than Happiness

Do you fill in spare time with activities which make you happy
Because you are not happy?
Do you do things you know are second rate to being happy
Because you know you are not happy?
Maybe it would be better
To look for what your happiness is inside you,
Not as an activity but being something else.

## The Crazy One

They will always wonder about the crazy one
Because he or she is the one with the cutting edge,
With the crazy unreasonable truths
They are too scared to explore.


## No Expert

When someone is treated like an expert,
It is because what they know is a tiny bit more about less.
There are usually many others who could have been asked
And done a good job.

It is good not to think or believe you are an expert
Even if you are treated like one
Because it makes you think harder
And then you go deeper and further than experts.


## Inside Out

I didn't want all the toys the others had.
They didn't appeal to what was inside
And I wasn't sure what did,
Until one day it arrived and found it was inside.


## Enemies as Friends

It is good to wander into your enemies' territory
Where you are treated with respect and openness.
Willing to learn what they have to teach you about yourself,
You can leave more freely.

## For You

Find your own instructions, even if you pinch some of these.
Yours are the only ones that you will see work for you.
Mine sometimes work for me.
Everyone else's sometimes work for them.

## 29. KEEPING OUR BALANCE

### The Balance

Why are we so complicated,
Full of things that don't necessarily sit together easily?
Let me speak for me first.
I look for inner peace, yet at the same time,
I seem critical of injustice.
I am detached from most,
But passionate about their loss of rights.
I will protect the defenceless even if it results in the offender
Suffering from seeing
What they tried to impose on the defenceless.

### Ships

A ship between two shores before a storm needs land.
One shore let go, the other beckons with its hand.
In some ways they are like us.

To sail at sea confirms the haven of land,
Which is not where ships should be.
Ships are most themselves at sea.

Nightly they leave one port,
Then silently arrive at another before dawn,
Always giving their best, like us not knowing what is next.

### Fully Empty Room

What a sense of joy when no egos are in a crowded room.
Thoughts pushed away,
Compassion is to all and stillness reigns.

## With Just Today

To be happy is everyone's desire
Because it is what we spend all our time trying to be.
We try so many different ways in all sorts of permutations.
There are some who are lucky and realise
They are happy just with what they have today
And don't need anything else.

## Silence Sings On and On

The last time we saw Patrick he was saying goodbye
From outside his ex-council house beside Glastonbury Tor.
With the Tor he had found a hill to live on the lower slopes of,
So that he could be on an upward mountain path.
His fatal condition brushed aside
To show us how he finished inside,
A person true to himself, a person who knew himself.

The last time I saw Patrick on my own,
He was waiting for death to arrive,
Meditating upright in the middle of a hospital bed.
I wanted to sing aloud to him the chant of the sacred mountain
But without saying a single word, instead,
We silently sung the same internal song.
Old friend your body has gone, but I see
We will not be forgotten for ignoring our thinking,
Because our silent stillness sings on and on.

## Keeping Thoughts Away

Keeping thoughts away is not what we are used to doing.
Saying no to thought is not what we are taught.
But when we see thoughts cause most misery,
We start keeping them away to make us happy.

## Clarity

When you know stillness, there is nothing to say about it.
Nothing can make it clearer than being still.

## Mountain Paths

When you seem down and have fallen over,
Get up where you fall,
Even if for half a step you have to crawl.

Mountains don't let you leap up their side;
They give you a choice to let you slowly grow inside.

Every wrong path you take, every mistake you seem to make
Are all progress on the inner mountain path.

Whilst you camp on the inner mountain path,
Sometimes clinging, sometimes singing,
Every pause, when there seems to be no change,
Are growths of inner silent strength.

## Continued Presence

When you are home,
There is nowhere to go on a pilgrimage to be happier.
You can only continue to turn inwards to be happy at home.

## Already There

Our growth is not what it seems.
It is mainly within,
Unseen because it is seeing what we already are.

## That Within

No matter how long we live or where we live,
We still have to surrender to that within.

## Total Eclipse

How much can we talk of happiness?
How much can there be?
Always never ending is best as it continues
To totally eclipse all misery.

## To be Happy

Do not underestimate the skill required
To ignore the negative in life to make you happy.
It takes up most of your life.

## Monopoly

No one has a monopoly on anything
Apart the nature of their inner self.

## Changing Attitude

Attitudes can be changed but sometimes until they are,
We cannot move anywhere.
Stuck we continue to wonder why.
It is good to ask yourself, 'Do I need to change my attitude?'

## Full

Have you tried being full of emptiness
So you are fully empty?

## Detaching but with others

Living attached to others, it can be impossible to be in solitude.
Living detached you can be in solitude
But be with all people if you choose.

## Master or Servant

The inner territory can be guessed.
We can have an opinion about it.
We can read about it and think we know it
Or we can surrender, serve it and be it.

## Triple Triad

We are known for our possession of things,
Our indifference to things, or our lack of things,
Especially money, power and ego,
And most importantly, simplicity, humility and compassion.

## Our Inner Room

It is our choice what we have.
In the room we choose to live in,
Our responsibility is to change it if we want.

**Stick with What You Like**

Only buy what you like, what you need, what you want.
Don't buy to have something because of its value to others.
It will only make you unhappy.


**Neither One Nor the Other**

Not everything that is wrong can be made right
Because they are the same; only on the other side.

Right and wrong like light and dark
Need each other to exist like men and women
Only exist because of the other.


**No More**

Eventually we know we can't be more happy
Or more thankful than we are.


**With Those**

Being away, what is missed the most
Is not the surroundings or your things
But the company of those you trust, those people.

The conversations which take you on a journey
Are only because everyone knows you for who you are.
No one is trying to impress you
And they only stick with you until they have to go.

It is where we all want to be again, back with those,
Back in that group, back on our own with them.

## Stopping to Ponder the Wonder of Time

Today is a mystery now and it won't happen again.
I don't yet know and it can never be repeated.
I will remember it but it has not yet happened.
How incredible is that?


## Exchange Clearly

When you are taking but in disguise of giving,
Don't try and make it look like someone
Doesn't want what you are offering.
Be honest.

If you want something; ask for it.
If you don't want something; say so.
If you want to exchange; say it.
If you are happy; share it.


## The Basket

So many people stay together because of the basket.
The basket is not worth anything on its own,
Only what they have put in it.
They only stay together because of what's in the basket.
Sometimes what is in the basket is more important
Than all the reasons they joined together.


## Happiness and Harm

There is nothing wrong with desiring what is natural.
Happiness is our natural state.
No one can be criticised for being happy being their self,
Except if it harms them or others.

## Homemade Love

I remember a birthday meal I spent in a supermarket carpark,
In a car on my own, savouring delicious food.
Today on the eve of my birthday,
I sat in another car park of that chain of supermarkets.

But I won't be there tomorrow because I will be at home,
Not in a car park of a strange town I once lived in,
But where I live with homemade food and homemade love.
My traveling work done.


## This is as Good as it Gets

Perhaps in just one of these moments
I will be happy with my truth or perhaps I am already,
But don't admit it.

Then, knowing I am, stops the search.
Stopping the search ends any potential happiness of hope.
Yes this is as good as it could ever be.
There is no hope for anything better.


## Understanding

How can anything else apart from madness
Truly understand madness?
How can anything else apart from having lived
Truly understand life?
How can anything else apart from mourning
Truly understand mourning?
How can anything else apart from receiving
Truly understand giving?
How can anything else apart from being loved
Truly understand love?

## 30. ENOUGH PAIN

### Pain

How much more pain do I want?
When will I stop saying yes to pain?
When will I stop staying in this trance?
With a threshold of no unnecessary pain
How can I see them again?
Detachment is the only way. No more to worry, to think or say.


### Enough Pain

Our families sometimes they appear to make us look smaller,
Just so we might grow taller.
Never passing you a compliment.

When you really needed someone there,
They made sure they were there,
Always doing something, just giving you time.

You never give up on them as you know they exist for you.
Except for them you would not exist.

The one thing they teach you is to see what you are,
Where you came from and no matter what, to respect this.

They showed you to stop anything
When you've had enough pain.
No point in going back for more, again, again and again.

Then you see that they showed you
How to pass on what you know and all you have to give:
Kindness, humility and simplicity.

## Apologies

Forgiving and apologising are never forgetting.
They mean always remembering
So we don't make the same mistake.

Apologising often expects more understanding
Than may be possible.
Accepting an apology
Often expects more understanding than may be possible.

## Anger and Honour

Anger can rapidly grow into violence because of
Lack of the experience, training and skill
To express an alternative opinion in a more constructive way.

To reel the neck in may need sensitivity and education,
To allow overriding of provoked impulsive responses,
And instead, aligning with honour of our own kind.

## Arguments

Don't get in the ring
Because there are some people best left alone,
Especially people who want a fight.

A bun fight is always best over real cake,
Instead of childish clever arguments,
Which should embarrass them into being adults.

To reel the neck in by a small step
Back from the furnace of emotions is triggered
By a simple thought which extinguishes all fire.

## Don't Get in the Ring

Most people will get in the ring
And have an argument with you, even if you don't know them.
Because we fall for it so easily,
We have to be more on our guard, so just don't get in the ring.

If you don't get in the ring,
You won't get psychologically mugged,
And you will begin to feel better,
So don't get in the ring.

Start by saying to the other person,
'You are right.' then keep on saying,
'You are right, you are right,'
Just don't get in the ring.


## 3 R's to remember Instead of Roaring

Don't get in the Ring.
Reel you neck in.
Say to the other, you are Right, and keep saying you are Right.


## Don't Step in the Ring

The problem with relationships is never the other person,
It's always us.
If you blame someone you are blaming, so talk or walk.
If you dislike someone and can't see love for them, fly or cry.
If you argue with someone you have chosen to get in the ring,
So step back out or get knocked out.
If you resent someone you may think you want them to die
But it is you who has taken the poison, so spit or smile.
When you can't get what you want,
See what you actually have, then see it again.

## Stillness is all we Are

We are always up against it,
Difficult people trying to get us in the ring,
Trying to engage us to spar with them,
But it only disturbs your peace.
So many times we find ourselves sparring
And before we know it,
We have been lured into the ring.
Remember constantly your happiness
And that stillness is all we are,
Then your guard is easier to keep up.


## Pass By

If you play games, I may appear to behave peculiarly.
I won't answer your notes or return your calls.
Making a game out of how you get on is not ok.
I can't waste today so I'll detach, move to the side,
Stay inside and let you pass by.


## Psychologically Mugged

I've got to stop this now as I've been hurt so many times.
I've had enough pain
And I don't want more from them ever again.

I've given them too many chances
And every time I got mugged.
I didn't acknowledge the emotional pain
But now my feelings can't be mugged again.

This is being clear about me doing things, so I don't get hurt.
It is not about helping anyone else's pain.
It is about me not getting mugged again.

## Overwhelming Situation

The overwhelming pain of loss of a person you love
Has no equal
Except if it happens again with another person you love.
Monstrously out of control feelings
Wash over fragile circuits of thinking, then there is standstill.

Sometimes all that is needed is a rest from the machinery,
Trying to work out what can only be worked through.
With rest is some peace, some time for silence,
So stillness inside can be uncovered.

## Being Selfish about Self Care

When will you say you have had enough pain,
That you don't just want to be the giver again?

When will you say they are not going to take off you again?
When will you think of you first and say no?

When will you say no they can't come and stay?
When will you say I've had enough, today is the day?

When will you wake up how you went to sleep
And say yesterday was the first day of me saying no?

No becomes the most positive word.
It changes the uncomfortable feeling inside
Into positive feelings of protecting yourself.

You start looking for times to say no,
Just to feel better about saying yes to you.
Then you see why so many people do it all the time and say no.
It makes them feel good.

## Natural Order

Avoidance of pain is our first response.
Desiring happiness is next.
After seeing the world, suffering is seen.
What follows is finding happiness inside.


## Move On

When you've had enough discomfort,
Too much pain from being a punch bag,
You see you can't do it again.
It could be after much change in a family or job.
Seeing the things you can't change,
The time has come for you to move on.


## No Expectations

How much bad behaviour do we take before we say no?
How much pain do we have to endure before we say no?

Our thinking doesn't work fast enough to save us from others,
Because we have too much trust in our own expectations.

## 31. KINDNESS

### The Three Important Things

What people are and what they do
Does not make as big an impression on us
As how they make us feel.

The novelist Henry James wrote,
"Three things in human life are important:
The first is to be kind; the second is to be kind;
And the third is to be kind."

### Authenticity

Kindness with simple disciplined good manners and respect
Make me feel better and civilised.
I don't want a gold star experience of anything
Without authenticity.

### Be a Donor of Kindness

Don't be a consumer be consumed
By giving away Inner wealth.
Be extravagant with humility, intoxicated with serenity.
Be true, be still, be you.
Be silent, be quiet, be self-reliant. Be kind, be strength.

### Strength

Be true. Be still. Be you.
Be silent. Be quiet. Be self-reliant.
Be kind. Be silent Be strength.

## Kindness Above all else

Gentleness and kindness
Are now not our first reactions to many people.
Instead, defensive actions have become automatic ,
Thinking that they will save us from
The wishes of aggressive people.

Kindness is always a better reaction
But is faked by those who want to use us.
They can leave us distrustful of genuineness,
Fearful of kindness itself.

Because kindness can be the most powerful thing
Which changes how we feel and how we see our world,
We can't let other people take our kindness away,
So we must never stop.
Being kind is the most important thing you can be.


## A Secret Life

She kept to herself and none of the things
Which she quite liked in shops or magazines
Ever found their way into her life
Because her gratitude for being happy made her
Generous with her smile and with the warmth from her heart.

When it could be kept as a secret,
She gave everything she could away.
A life full of happiness, passed without incident,
Without a flicker of notice. She was here then gone,
But perhaps she is waiting to be found in you.

## 32. EXPECTATIONS

### Expectation

Those who expect nothing remain disappointed.
Those who have nothing can lose it when they get something.
Better to expect getting something to lose.

### Destiny

Immersion in the vast sea of our apparent interconnectedness
In family or in work can easily drown us,
So we are overwhelmed and can no longer be detached.
We get drawn in, lured in and tempted.
It is better to be a brief visitor like a holiday maker on vacation,
Detached from destinations but not destiny.

### Letting Go of Expectations

What has gone? Our expectations, our hopes and dreams,
Or our reluctance to let her be whatever she is no matter what.

We can only help her with the tools
To do whatever she is going to do.
Perhaps show her how to be still,
To give her the strength to endure it.

### Accomplishments

Being alive to what can be accomplished
Means not doing unnecessary things
And focusing on what needs to be done,
What possibly can be done, so that all we can do is done.

## Trust

I trust me because I can't pretend I trust anyone
Because anyone can let you down, even if they don't intend to.

You can be set up to compete
Without knowing that you are competing
Or you can set yourself up.
That is why I trust me even if I am wrong.


## Entertainment

I am not an entertainer and I realised this
When as a boy of twelve my magic tricks didn't work,
So I decided there was no point in just being a fake.

That I can't entertain is due to lack of confidence
Because I am not amusing. I am not an amusement.
I am happiest being my own self.


## Our Expectations

They would understand what I have done
But I don't know if they would agree with me
Or if they would have done it if they were me.
But they are not me.

They gave me life but I have to choose what to do with it
As those after me will.
Inheritance is a mistake
Because its expectations pressurise decisions.
It is best to let someone be what they are.

## Unconditional

When you don't live from your head,
Everything is unconditional.
Your self does not have conditions because you are just you.


## Unconditionality

When the last dependable person is not here,
The only unconditional person in life seems to be you
But what you think you are can let your self down or save you.

## 33. POSITIVITY

### Dodging the Negative

You can keep drinking bitterness
And keep chewing on resentment,
Searching for hooks to hang them on,
Trying to find a person to say you are right.

Or you can dodge the negative getting in your light,
Keeping it to the side of you,
So you can see your light.
You don't need to fish for compliments.

### Some Days

Some days don't seem to be for happiness.
Some days we have to write.
Some days we have to walk.
Some days we have to be silent,
But all of these let us be happy.

### Divinely Inspired

What we do anywhere, no matter what it is,
If it comes from inside our self,
It comes from what we see as the divine.

### More Important to be Nice

You may be the best at a game, the best at the arts,
But one day someone will emerge who is the same.
The only difference may be that they or you are nice.

## Risk of Pain

Occasionally you have to let yourself feel bad for a while,
Without letting it last too long.
Sometimes you have to feel how bad it has got
And only then you decide to change it.

You don't want to look for pain
But you also don't want to avoid the possibility of it,
Because if you don't experience the possibility of pain,
You cannot experience the possibility of the alternative.

## Listening Kindness

Listening to the inner self,
Keeping the ego in check in stillness,
The inner person is heard.
Listening to the inner self
Is the greatest kindness you can receive.

## Not From the Head

You get a lot more peace
When you live from the heart not the head,
From the soul not the head, from the self not the head.
The heart, soul or self or whatever you call you,
Does not have conditions.

## My Contribution

What am I bringing to the table, to the relationship,
To the problem to solve it, to life to make me happy?
We can only bring our self.

**From inside**

Whichever way you can see it, it doesn't matter
As seeing, hearing and feeling are only pointing
Back from where they came from, inside.


**Bathed in Light**

I remember, so can you, clear sunny days,
Everything bathed in sunlight, everyone bathed in sunlight.
Is there any difference in anything, everyone
Or the sunlight or is it the way it is seen?


**Art World View**

Our work and view of the world
Is like the artist and the canvas;
The canvas should not paint the artist.


**Positivity**

It is possible to write about things other than happiness
But why write about things which we don't want?
It is better to write about what we want,
What we can't see and how to get them
Rather than to look at what we don't want?

It is equally important to read, discuss
And see what stops us being happy
And what helps us be happy.
There is no point in reading, discussing
And seeing what makes us unhappy.
It will only make us more unhappy.

## Isn't it Great That

Isn't it great that darkness can be removed. Isn't it great that.
Isn't it great that happiness follows suffering. Isn't it great that.
Isn't it great that happiness is inside. Isn't it great that.
Isn't it great that anyone can be happy. Isn't it great that.
Isn't it great that it is free. Isn't it great that.

## 34. CREATIVITY

### Stemming the Tide of Rationalism

Early experiences of distressing thoughts and feelings
Are sometimes only healed later by correcting the errors
Through drawing, painting, sculpting, singing, music, writing,
Communicating our love, friendship and kindness.

### Process Over

What you or I could communicate, which is little,
Has already been and gone.
The present has arrived and is here,
With time for peace, consciousness of today is precious.

### Artists and Their Material

Meeting artists is like meeting musicians,
As they are usually not like anything which they present,
And why should they be
Because they have taken a tortuous route to contort,
Not resort to what we take for granted.

### Failure

Failure is one of the best motivators
And the best place to start from time and time again,
As failure is always available.

Failure is begging for change, begging for improvement.
Failure has the greatest potential,
More potential than success.

## Artists

Picasso showed where inside his true colours came from
As his obsession with the female form
Pushing his genius to its end,
His art slightly around the bend like us.

Gaudi's art's offspring everywhere in his buildings
Are asking you to speak, to respond to,
And rejoice in the artist's reflection of nature.


## Spiritual Love

The best words worth reading, the best poems worth writing,
The best songs worth hearing are natural,
Those of spiritual love.


## Creativity

Inspiration rarely comes from nowhere.
Usually you think you might be able to do something better
Or just dare yourself to solve a problem
Or show it in a different way.
Then, falling asleep or engaged in something ordinary,
You find yourself on a pathway
Which has just opened up in front of you.
You are conscious you are on your own and feel alone
With a hundred thousand pairs of eyes looking down on you,
Wanting to look up at you.

## Happy Work

We become so fixated on what we decide to do,
We can forget to enjoy the moments
From the decision until we actually achieve it,
And the pleasure of work is gone.


## Being Shown

The person I knew has gone. They have been taken over,
Their holiday is now spent,
Compelled to sing, draw or write in silence
Whatever comes into the heart or into the mind.
That which seems important has to be written sung or drawn.
No sleep in to be lazy because it is life's work being shown.


## Anti-perfection

Taking risks, the mistakes are not mines trying to destroy you,
But only there to encouraging progress.
Taking risks leaving any forgiveness behind,
Exploring what is not explored lets you expand your mind.
Perfection is the enemy of progress
As it stifles looking further, halting all growth,
Progress with imperfection is the growth process.
Imperfection is human which is your friend.


## Art is Us

All the best songs, poems and art are not about us. They are us.
Songs sing only of our love for others in our self.
Poems speak of our love of the world in our self.
Art displays to others the love we could have for our self.

## Pain of Art

We seem like such creatures of habit
But only in some things, some times.
We go for the same breakfasts, stay with the same people.

Our minds are conditioned from the past
That make the future secure,
Predictable, paradisiacal, comfortable
With no inconvenience, discomfort or pain.

Only artists are forced to experiment
With themselves and their art.

Some are already but some become what their art will show.
Comfort is stifling, so fear of discomfort is turned into fuel
To go even further, to see what happens where they can go.

Some can sing the love. Some can paint the pain.
Some can sculpt a hole so deep
It seems like you'll never get out again.

But there are those who imagine what we can only dream
And they directly show our eyes
What our hearts have not yet seen.


## Illusion of Songs

I used to believe in songs.
I used to love anthems of our lives of our times.
But these come and go like the people driven to write the lines
Who are simply part of our growing up and moving on too.

To have what the singer says you can find,
You can't as they say 'keep on becoming.'
You have to stop and be still.

### Radiate

Silently radiate like a still eagle, like a small ray of light,
And influence is yours.


### Curves

The straight line is a curse and of all the lines is the worst.
It has to be straight not bent or with an angle
And not allowed to droop or dangle.
It ruins the line of things which could be curved
And better for the eye to observe.
The body has got no straight lines.
Nature is not sophisticated to be so poorly defined.


### The Best Light

It's not even breakfast yet and most of my day's work is done.
All the thinking is gone. The day to enjoy is now here.

Artists know the early morning light is best
Because few people get out of bed to see it.

It looks more unusual,
Simply because the light comes from the other side.

The morning is best to see most things
As the night brings shadows of fear, illusions
Which are only clear again in the morning light.

## The Arts

The moodiness of the poet made me moody with you,
And you showed me how you have other sides too.
I guess the poet seems like no hero but instead like a soldier,
They try to show us things no one else can see.

It's not the paint or the brush that outlines the love;
It's the stroke of the hand
Which weaves the story from the heart.
It's only the presence of the heart
We see in the stoke of the hand
That draws or writes
And the presence of the heart we hear on the lips that sing.


## Imperfectly Beautiful

Honouring our brokenness and happiness
Is like seeing a broken pot
Repaired with gold dust in the glue,
So all the breaks are visible.

The gold cracks show that when repaired
With all its scars visible,
The imperfect piece of pottery may be more beautiful
Than the perfect original.

It can be a restorative process
Representing a changed perspective,
Of healing and wholeness
Accepting the imperfectly beautiful.

## 35. DIFFICULT PEOPLE

### Passive Aggression

Telling someone they are stressed out, or they are angry
Are none of your business if you are not going to help
Because if you tell someone without offering help,
You are making them think about you, not them.
It is all about you and so you have become the problem.

### Dark Triad

When relating to someone is strained,
With lack of agreeableness and conscientiousness,
Try and remember to think of
The triple personality the Dark Triad.

For success their Machiavellianism uses charm
To interpersonally manipulate everyone
As they are unprincipled masters of deception.

Their Narcissism makes them seem superior
Even grandiose
But they overdress to look good.

Their psychopathic coldness
But impulsive love of danger,
Sees them take risks in leading.

The one in a hundred people with the Dark Triad personality
Will exploit and take every opportunity
To get what they want no matter what. Watch out.

## Keeping the Main Aim the Main Aim

A sustained attack of thoughts lasting one month
Can be so distracting; so consuming,
It can take you to your limits of coping.

It can be any distraction from another person,
Someone challenging you or stealing from you,
Who you can't formally stop, someone who plays a game.

Their game interferes with your control of thoughts.
Keeping a steady aim as things continue,
Your victory is more certain than you can see.

Keeping the outer aim steady, retreat inside.
Find inner stillness and silence and let this overwhelm all.
Slowing the breath will eventually slow the thoughts,
Keeping the main aim the main aim.


## Making Someone Look Stupid

Making someone feel stupid
Is a wounding that must not go unchallenged.
Telling others doubles the wound and doubles the violence.

Making someone feel stupid
Is a wounding that must not go unchallenged.
To understand their error in the abuse of authority.

Making someone feel stupid
Is a wounding that must not be repeated
As no opportunity for a second chance should exist.
It's a terminal event.

## Compelled

A crook needs to be crooked to succeed.
They are like this because
They don't know how to be happy being straight.

They can create gossip and smokescreens
To hide what they are really like.
They can present as honestly doing good
When it is all part of their acting.

If you don't play their game
Or don't play with them and you are not playful,
They have to find another playmate,
Because they are compelled by what they are.


## Un-negotiate

You cannot negotiate to make meaningful progress
With certain types of people,
Because even inevitable, painful consequences
May not move them.
If they keep on coming back,
They usually need to be firmly told.


## Caution

People who use and abuse others approach them
With friendliness, promises and kindness not hostility.
Once fooled, because we are sensitive, we train to be
Defensive, cautious and guarded in how we respond
As we can still be fooled, attacked and destroyed.
We need strong unmovable defences.

## Best Teacher

The most cunning, sadistic, greedy,
Selfish, dishonest, wealthy person
With no principles
Taught me more than anyone about what I want.


## Obituary

Why not give obituaries to people when they are alive,
When it could have the most meaning, the most impact?
Why wait until they are dead?

Perhaps it is a way of having power over them
And their mistakes,
A judgement which they do not hear.
Perhaps obituaries are rude, cruel, vengeful
And are having the last word.


## Trusted

Not trusting is the most important thing
To learn about everyone else.
Not trusting is the most difficult thing
Because it is learnt only through pain
Received from trusting someone.
Not trusting is vital for survival, vital for enthusiasm
Because you have to trust only you.


## I don't want to spend an evening with

My teachers, my siblings,
My customers at work,
The prime minister, president the king or queen.

## Intangible

We are refugees in a world which is still trying to get rid of us,
A world which does not support the contemplative life,
A world where there have to be results.
The intangible is becoming the rarest of all.
It needs protecting the most to pass on.


## Protecting Dangerous Beauty

There is no rescue from life as being alive is dangerous
And only we can protect our self.
If we stop, the danger increases.

No one else can rescue us from life
Because we are meant to be here.
We have been placed here by people to live this dangerous life.

Protecting our self from depending on other's protection
And doing it our self brings peace
To this dangerous beautiful life.


## Mental Health and Personality Disorder

Realising a childhood friend you knew is not actually well
Is sad and at the same time a loss.
Expectations are different as they can't travel the same distance
And be with you the rest of your journey.
Although you never stop loving them as a friend,
The parting has already happened, the friendship changed.

## Intolerability

Intolerable situations can be other people
Imposing aspects of their lives on ours,
So that our life is unhappy or not fulfilling our self.
Either we change and move or they do.

## Securities, Power and Ego

Whatever I have done or not but others say I have,
Is their thinking.
It is known by me but thought by others.

Whatever I have been or not but others say I have,
Is their thinking.
It is known by me but thought by others.

Other's investment in judging me
May enrich their world of securities
Or may make it look like they overpower me
Or make their ego greater.

Inner happiness with our past overrides other's investments.
It is legitimate permission to be happy now, harmonious,
Not striving for power, ego or securities.

## Justice

I don't believe scales balance sides.
I don't believe blindfolds objectively see.
I don't believe the sword punishes.
There is no right side and there is no justice.
They are only words.
There is however consciousness of deliberate intent
To destroy what is not theirs to even touch.

## Illusion

Perhaps we need to look again and make sure we are sensitive,
Not uneducated or inexperienced,
Just not willing or able to accept dishonest as honest
Or cruel as kind.

Perhaps we need to look again
And make sure we are not willing or able
To accept being smart as coming from the heart,
Religion as spirituality or duty as compassion.

Perhaps we need to look again
And make sure we are not willing or able
To accept hearing as listening or seeing as looking,
Thinking as understanding or doing as being.


## Mindlessness

I told them not to be mindful, not to run mindfulness courses,
Not to write mindfulness books
But to be mindless.

They could only see their thoughts.
They didn't try to see without them.
They couldn't see stillness, couldn't be without their thoughts.

Now they have to cope
With running corporate industrial mindfulness courses,
Supporting the thinking which produces the very reactions
They were meant to help recover from with mindfulness.

## Religious Organisations and the Self

If you are part of an organisation,
You have to be loyal to it as you represent it.
If you only have yourself,
You have to be loyal to you as you represent yourself.

Being loyal to an organisation means helping to maintain it
And may require concealment, collusion and coldness,
For the greater good.
Being loyal to honesty, simplicity and kindness in yourself,
There is nothing greater or better.


## Ignored

Being ignored means not being regarded
With enough importance.
Being ignored means not being taken seriously enough.

Being ignored means manners are not being heeded
As a statement.
Sometimes it is best to ignore being ignored,
Sometimes it is the end.


## Minding Yourself

I tend to stay away from people as they can cause
Unimaginable trouble which you could not make up.

If you have not had enough trouble,
Mix in until you are in too much trouble,
Perhaps then you will mind yourself.

## Passionate Nature to Injustice

My passionate reactive nature is from my parents
And some people find it too much, but it doesn't worry me
Because it is only me trying to speak.

I have seen injustice and I have had injustice.
It is incorrect not to act, not to speak,
And if ignored, to not act and speak repeatedly.

I am frequently left a little disappointed
Others don't trust my over-passionate nature
Which is just like tuned up hearing.


## My Opponent

Our opponents are our best teachers,
So what did mine teach me?
They showed me I am still passionate about what I do.

Through betrayal, dishonesty and gossip,
An opponent can ignore responsibilities and abuse power,
So it becomes a force against you, weakening you
Or correcting and strengthening your weaknesses.

It is good to be passionate about integrity,
About being kind, about not being late, about respect.

It is good to be passionate about not lying,
About being direct, open and honest,
About simplicity, about hard work.

## Your Opponent

Your opponent is always your best teacher,
Your best friend and often a hidden part of you.

Treat your opponent with more respect, above everyone else,
As they can teach you more
If you find out why they oppose you.

They may lay down their life to show you this.
Even though you cannot see this,
You cannot exist fully without them.


## Higher Ground

When you are troubled,
Stand back from the waves trying to crash on you
And take one step backwards up the shore.

Getting to higher ground,
Keep on stepping backwards,
Getting higher from the waves.

Finding yourself on higher ground,
Let go of everything lower down.
Look around you, seeing everything that makes you happy.

Enjoy the happiness on higher ground,
The silence, the stillness.
This is where you belong.


## Leave Them Alone

Leave those alone who don't want your help
As they will be looked after by their self or someone.

## No Change Wanted

I'm so unchallenged today,
I had to give up helping people to change
Because they don't want to change.

I walked away from that because it made my batteries flat,
Disappointed but not defeated, my calmness intact.

Courage is not on tap but comes from a challenge
And we are not ready until it passes this way.

## Professor Troubles

What you don't like, what troubles you, what makes you upset,
That is your best friend, your best teacher, your own professor.

The best teacher is the reaction inside you,
Wanting you to see you may need to change your attitude
To the best expert on you, and listen to your internal advisors.

## Change or Leave

Yes it is correct, since stopping working for me,
I've not been able to stay in a job for long.
Three months to two years was the best of forty
And if I worked the next forty, nothing would change.

When I find out what's happening I cannot collude,
So when placed in a position where I change or speak,
I have had to speak and leave.

It has never been a problem for me to speak and walk away
And I have always been able to sleep at night,
Even now out in the cold, I am warm inside.

## Stream of Jobs

My work has always been short term jobs.
Eventually when I've seen my colleagues,
I've not been able to collude with them
So I have always had to leave.

When I tried to oppose their conduct to protect the defenceless
They had the reins of power; I had the path to the door.

I have my foolishness.
Theirs was exchanged
For pensions and comfortable retirement long ago.
Integrity is not often comfortable or respected.


## Be Quiet

Unless you know something they don't,
Don't say it unless they ask
And even if you do know something they don't,
Don't say it until they ask again.


## Complex Mankind

We are walking collections of interactive, integrated,
Complicated experiences
Ready and waiting to be explained simply.
We are happy to baby sit a lion cub.
Happy to process information on computers.
Happy to work for peace.  Happy to help.
Happy to love and happy to die.

## Refugee

Go to that place, the one you know as a refuge from outside,
Where you shine brightest in silence.

You will not let yourself down
By having time and concentration
Until unity and happiness are uncovered once more.


## Integrity

Usually in the thick of it we can't see what it was we started
By what appeared like a small decision to stand our ground.

Complexity does not diminish our integrity.
Secrecy and deception only highlight it.


## Detaching from Overthinking

When we overthink,
Detachment is separating ourselves from others.
Detachment is separating our processes
From other people processes.

Detachment is separating our thoughts
From other people's thoughts.
Detachment is separating our feelings
From other people's feelings.


## Someone Special

Some days have almost everything
You could have thought of to be perfect,
Then you are surprised because someone makes you happier.

## Changing On Our Own

There are periods of deep inner change
Which may not yet be worked out in thoughts,
So there is unrest, unhappiness, worry
And we are often alone until it is processed.

Processing change can't be rushed even if it is instant change,
Because accommodation to the change
Has to be met on every level, and has its own time.

On our own, our thoughts transform into words
What we want to say.
Only then, how we will live our days can be worked out.

## Recovery of Your Own Life

Recovery of your own life may never occur
But like a car crash,
A crisis is usually the best thing to ever happen,
To get back what you lost and ditch the unnecessary.

Reclaiming and restoration of feelings, of clear thinking,
Of balance, of health can then be returned.

Reclaiming and restoration of friendship,
Of strength, of hope, of the spirit can then be returned.

## Mind Your Own Business

If it is none of your business, leave it alone.
It is none of your business what other people think about you,
So just be you.

## Joy and Problems

The joy and problems we have with others,
Are a function of living with others and do not go.
The joy and problems we have with our self,
With being in the world do not go.
Both joy and problems with others, our self
And just being happy with our self are being vibrantly alive.


## Skip Once a Day

With everyone and everything, ask what is good.
Life is a range of many different experiences.
A smile, a child, a stranger waving to you on the road,
Daydreaming, making a new friend.
Skip one step a day like a child.


## Whose Stuff

When you leave your family it can be the right thing.
You can continue to lovingly grow together
Seeing and being with each other.

Some families are dangerous company and you have to escape.
Some are so distressed and incapable,
They dump you somewhere.

Some families stop you getting on and won't let you leave,
So when they keep on pulling you back,
It may be time to talk or separate.

We have to find our own life, letting them continue theirs.
Giving them their stuff and dealing with ours,
Gives us freedom to let all our lives blossom.

## Keep Busy

Everything comes with its own appointment.
Answers come in their time, not ours.
We can't change allotted appointments
Because we want satisfactory answers.
Just being occupied whilst waiting for the answer
Ensures we are ready for whatever it gives us.

## People Problem Algorithm

People problems have a process.
First there is a problem, then an awareness
And then thinking about it as a problem.

Then there is acceptance,
Then the question of whose problem is it.
Then there is who should deal with it, then letting them know.
Then letting go.

## Not Just a Piece of Kit

We are all pieces of kit
And we perform various functions in different settings.
We move from one setting to the next
And someone takes our place,
Like we took someone else's before.
We know our place and worth,
But sometimes not the timing of where we are supposed to be.
Sometimes we choose, sometimes others do
But we are much more than what we do.
We are a piece of kit for that setting,
But we live and love in many settings.

## Be Direct and Clear

Always ask yourself what do you want from you today.
It is not what is usually asked,
But if it is not asked at the beginning
It will always have to be asked at the end.
Instead, people mention in passing with a hint or a sigh
That you seem busy today and so it is not important.
Manipulation is a game only two can play
So shooting first, asking questions later is the only way to play.


## Mental Washing

Reprograming ourselves has to be done every day,
If we let ourselves be programmed by information
From people, the media,
Selling of everything by everyone.

Reprogramming ourselves every night,
Like washing our faces
Of all the dirt we have accidently picked up,
Is essential to keep us our authentic self.


## Eclipsed

Big egos in the room, jostling for importance
Are totally eclipsed by one person's inner stillness.


## Yourself

As knowing what it is to be a parent
Can only be known by being a parent,
So truth can only be known by being true to yourself.

## Ditch Stereotypes

The races, colours, religions we both share
Are conditioned learned thinking,
So let's do some unlearning, un-thinking.

All men want is just one thing sex.
All women want is men's money.
Black is bad, white is good. Cold is bad, warm is good.

Stop these in their tracks from blocking you being free to relate
To everyone by thinking and processing instead . . .

I'm Muslim get over it. I'm disabled get over it.
I'm a foreigner get over it.
I'm gay get over it. I'm lesbian get over it.
I'm LGBT get over it.
I'm black get over it. I'm old get over it. I'm in NA get over it.
I'm left wing get over it. I'm right wing get over it.
I'm Irish get over it.
I'm Welsh get over it. I'm Scottish get over it.
I don't have children get over it.
I'm British get over it. I'm Jewish get over it.
I'm American get over it.
I'm Hindu get over it. I'm Chinese get over it.
I'm Russian get over it.
I'm Christian get over it. I'm in AA, NA and GA, get over it.
I'm a loner get over it. I'm a weirdo get over it.
I'm abnormal get over it.


## Don't Give Your Happiness Away

Don't think about being happy. Just be happy.
Don't analyse being happy. Just be happy.
Don't give your happiness away by what others say.
Don't let anyone take your happiness away by what they say.

## Humanity

The quiet confidence
Of having the power of our teachers and ancestors
And openly sharing with the young as equals
Is humanity.

## Guilt Anger Consequences

Someone behaving badly affects me,
Then they make me feel awkward for telling them,
So I feel guilty.
They don't change,
But they try to turn my guilt into a problem,
So that I am the bad person.
As it is not my issue, I leave them to the consequences.

## Only the Small Mistakes Count

Permitting a small mistake can cost us dearly,
Because it is the denial of small mistakes which matter,
As the big ones are usually seen.

# 36. CHOICE AND OPPPORTUNITIES

## Choosing

We are distracted by being attracted
To complexity not simplicity,
To noise not silence, to movement not stillness,
To resistance rather than acceptance, to desire not happiness.

We are attracted to thinking rather than being still,
To importance not humility, to personality not principles,
To gaining rather than sharing, to looking out not in.

We are attracted to the future not the present,
To speech not the grace of silence, to style not content,
To competitiveness not cooperation,
To separateness not compassion.

We are attracted to distractions rather than non-attachment,
To seeing parts not everything, to the many not the few,
To the popular not the outsiders,
To dividing rather than bringing together.

We are attracted to mystery not truth, to doing not being,
To emotions not love, to power not friendliness.

In summary, we are attracted to complexity not simplicity,
To thinking rather than being still, to the future not the present,
To attachment rather than non-attachment,
To mystery not truth.

The essence is,
'Simply be still now non-attached true to the self.'

## Fist Inspired Passion

When did the rising of passion begin?
For me it was from the disappointment of my feeling
Of being ritually abused when that fist hit my face?

The teacher's pride was being an ex-Army Boxing champion.
In front of the whole school, lined up for games,
Each of the four blows lifted me off my feet.

Any defensive reaction to the first taste of abusive power
Would have been answered only by escalating pain ,
Losing my place at college.

Then he turned around to face them and shouted,
'That's for nothing, now try something.'

Self-preservation is escaping
Into a newly discovered inner land.
Diving further inside to the inner land,
Is the only place where peace and happiness is restored


## Missionaries

Helping others only helps you to help others
Which is not wrong.
Helping may not help them help themselves;
It may keeps them where they are,
Helping can be a selfish act to further your own ends.
Religion's missionaries know this best.

## Inner rules

See no hatred only the positive, overlooking other's faults.
Get on with your own life, leaving others' concerns alone.
Or see that what you do for someone, you really do for you,
So do it perfectly.

## Alternative Path to Psychiatry

I wanted to be able to give what I could give,
To show alternatives to suffering and pain
With kindness and compassion,
Which had little to do with psychology or psychiatry.
Wherever I was, I wanted most importantly
To be with a sense of the inner self, the spirit within.

## Reasons Why I Quit Training in Psychiatry

When I saw Over half of the psychiatrists were addicts.
Then when I saw few of the rest were mentally well.

Next was the treatment
Of a survivor of Auschwitz with depression.
When electroconvulsive therapy failed,
The psychiatrists advised her to have a frontal lobotomy.
My saying she had had enough torture was ridiculed.
And my connection with psychiatry was broken forever.

After I left I was reassured on hearing research evidence,
That for people with severe psychiatric disorders,
A six week stay in the Muthuswamy South Indian temple,
Doing light duties produced the same improvement
As a month of standard psychiatric treatment.

## Do You Want a Brew?

'The new water heater is better than that old kettle,'
The Psychotherapist said to the cleaner.
'Stays hot and saves me so much time.
I can pour a cup any time and get more work done.
The cleaner looked her in the eye
And saw the glint of self-importance.
'I prefer still using the old one, that's why I've kept it.
I can ask someone if they want a brew.
Then wait with them while it boils,
Spending that time together chatting
Or not breathlessly trying to save time.
There's nothing wrong with the old kettle.
No need to replace it.
Waiting for it to boil lets me calm my thinking,
So I'm not a servant to restlessness.'

## Only You

You only need to be true to you, only you.
There is no one else you need to be true to.
Not to the written word, neither to stories or books,
Nor to the world of comings and goings, only to you.
Not to the teacher, preacher or doctor,
Neither to subjects, only you.

## Involvement

Just because the majority supports a person,
Doesn't mean they are right.
A whole country can support something
And be wrong about it,
But be right about supporting each other.

## Choiceless Paths

Even though I ended up on the opposite path,
Which was my second choice, my second choice was the best.

My first choice was the best, then my second choice was.
They seemed different but now they are the same.
They can only merge into one path.

The point of breakthrough was seeing and realising
That the path I took was the right one all the time.

We can only see the road we are on not the one ahead.
The path we are on is the only one
That can lead to the one ahead.


## Predestination

Your thoughts are not original.
They are not your own unique thoughts.
They are common, quite usual thoughts
Which we have been having for thousands of years.

You think that your thoughts make you behave
Like you want to,
But are you sure?
Maybe you are going through the thinking motions
Which ensure what is supposed to happen will happen.

When we seem to choose, perhaps it was already so.
It is a belief that choice indicates no predestination.
But choice is not in truth optional. Truth is not a choice.

**Forever Young**

Brothers and sisters like to compete to find out
And show you who they are,
And by joining in you find more about you as well.

But as adults, not leaving things like this behind,
When there should be more serious things on their minds,
Is childish.

If the relationship is subtle combat,
And continues without development,
Eventually there is no choice but to leave and be with friends.

**Going Our Own Way**

Whichever way you go,
All paths lead you to the same final path.
Whichever way you go,
It will be on your own path, nobody else's path.
Your final path for you
Began so long ago and the choice never ends
To leave behind your happiness, your nature and your smile.

**The Outcome will Explain**

However odd I may seem.
However wrong in my choices, it is right just to be me.
There is a strange intuition behind my choices
I cannot explain; only the outcome can.

## Choosing Happiness

We can sit around doing nothing
Or we can sit around trying to be happy
By the only means we know.


## An Unfortunate Man

The Russian or American billionaire on their yacht,
With their seventeen crew,
Who can sail it to one of their mansions
Of coral bays, sand and surf and unhappiness are unfortunate.


## No Trace

Would you rather leave no trace or something of importance?
All traces will eventually go,
So do you want to spend time leaving a trace.


## Dropping Expectations

If we drop our expectations of someone,
Accepting them for what they are
And not trying to change them, we have less of a problem.

Dropping expectations doesn't lesson us,
But lets us grow wiser branches for others to settle on.


## Choose Wisely

It is easy not to be happy, so easy to be sad.
What persuades us is not worth more than us.

**So You Think You Choose**

Information you are given as a warning
Or guidance doesn't usually help,
Because it is your destiny that drives you, not your head.
Whatever you do leads you there.
Whatever you don't do leads you there, just the same.


**You Choose**

When you are young in your teens, you choose your nurturing,
What you feed off and live on.
You will remember this as it can be growth or decay.

To start with decay is only slight
But all the slight choices of decay add up
And as you start to feel unwell, others begin to notice.
You isolate yourself with your choices until everyone has gone.

To start with growth is only slight
But all the choices add up
And as you start to feel happy, others begin to notice.
Choosing solitude,
Your consciousness lets you be part of everything.

You choose your path from only two, decadence to decay or
growth to happiness.
You can live the life of either chaotic messy descent
Or the disciplined inner life of being consciously happy in
stillness.


**Impact**

Our pattern is not seen until we have nearly completed it,
Our impact usually not until we have gone.

## Appearance

Why do we appear to choose unwisely?
Are we copying someone, a parent, a hero a friend?
Do we choose suffering
Because we can see the reward is happiness?


## Acceptance Our Friend

Maybe everything is just as it should be
And we should stop thinking how to change it.
Non-acceptance can be our greatest enemy,
Acceptance our waiting friend.
If we accepted life we would have less to do,
More time for peace and more to just be.


## Don't Miss Opportunities

Don't miss opportunities to be kind.
Don't miss opportunities to be with friends.
Don't miss opportunities to be your self.
Don't miss opportunities to be happy.


## Visitors

We think we have control over our world
Because we want to have control over our world.
But we can also see our world has its own
Form, movement and intentions because it is not ours.

## To Adjust During the Inevitable

My friend Narikutti had a guru,
Yogaswami of Jaffna who used to say:
'All is truth.
There is not even one wrong thing.
We do not know.
It was all accomplished long ago.'

We are more powerless than we want to admit,
So surrendering helps us to be calm and composed
Producing an inner 'serenity of surrender.'

## 37. FATE

### The Hands of Fate

Sometimes I ask, 'What is worth making a decision about
When it was all decided long ago?'
Either way it will turn out how it was meant to be,
So a decision is made more easily.

### Complete Surrender to Fate

Even though we know and even though we are told,
Even though we read about it and see it all the time,
Death slowly becomes more surprising and acceptable
As time goes by.
Knowledge and health don't help accept it more.
They can both make the thought of it worse.
Perhaps complete surrender to fate
Is the only way to keep it at bay.

### Acceptance

Why should we be frightened of dying or death?
It is nature and fate letting us fulfil our purpose?
They cannot be changed from what they are letting us be;
What we are.

### Fate's Hand

When you are uninjured but others are not.
When you survive and others do not,
You cannot look at these incidents without fate having a hand.

## Only Words

Past and future are words we use to describe
Thoughts of what is.
Past and future are only words we use to understand fate.
Past and future are only words for fate.


## Your Journey

Eventually you see you have been following a scent.
You have been listening for truth.
You have been watching for it, waiting for it.
It is the stillness here inside you.

Then you see your journey has taken care of you,
The path leading to a place,
A river, a plain, a sacred mountain.
They are your stillness.


## Fate

Fate is not anything like a power in control.
It is not something that can be named.
Everything is fate and fate is everything.
Fate is what things are meant to be as they are.


## Our Life as a Fateful Play

A long drawn out play with the characters people we know,
Playing their parts with us.
Surprising us with their scripts and moves
Which seem written long before,
Because we already know the ending.

## Compelling

Compelled to live, compelled to be happy,
Compelled to be and not to be is our fate.


## Right on Time

Returning to stillness is our origin and fate.
Stillness is never early or late.


## Before In-between and After

Wave after wave of us fall and just like soldiers in denial
Who think,
'It won't be me,'
We think the same just to buffer our acceptance.

There are never any exceptions
To how fate is not just first and last
But everything before, in-between and after.

## 38. MIND CONTROL

### What We Eventually Find

You don't need a clever doctor.
You don't need a psychologist or psychiatrist.
You don't need anyone to tell you
That you need to control your own mind.
It is the simplest thing of all to miss
That can leave us all in a mess,
Not seeing we are responsible for being in control of our mind.

### Soul Mind

I am so happy I never valued thinking much
And never gave it control,
As my mind would have taken over the direction of my heart.

### Starting and Stopping

Just when I can't think of anything else
And I feel that's the day done,
Something crops up and it finds its life on a page.
How strange that consciousness lets thoughts form
Which search for words to become sentences
Which can be written spoken or forgotten.
Stopping them is also its main job.

### Most Powerful Medicine

Now is the time to be overwhelmed
By a daily dose of my favourite drug,
Taken each night at the same time; my sleep.

## The Drug of Drugs

There are no unwanted side effects.
No one else is involved.
You make a full recovery until you need more.
It sedates you and lets you sleep.
It gives you an altered state of consciousness,
The most natural drug of tiredness.

## Ignorance

In the West, what we don't know we call the unconscious,
In the East, we call it the ego.
Neither is right nor wrong only names for our ignorance.

## Without

With ignorance we are searching for happiness.
Without ignorance the search is called off.

With ignorance our thoughts are in control.
Without ignorance we are happy without them.

With ignorance we suffer in the outside world.
Without ignorance we are happy inside.

With ignorance we have not surrendered.
Without ignorance surrender is complete.

With ignorance we are busy in the world.
Without ignorance we have detached.

## Levels of Attainment

Some people seem to wake and change in their teens.
Others in their twenties, thirties or in a late decade.
But when darkness is removed and they wake up,
Ignorance has started to go.

There are different levels of attainment,
As some have only one eye slightly open.
The lucky few have both eyes slightly open
And most rare, someone who has one eye fully open.
When limited sight is present for some ,
There is only one purpose left,
The desire to see completely, to have ignorance fully removed.

## To Be Still in Happiness

You will have a certain attitude to want
To be in a special place for detachment, solitude and silence.
But to enquire, surrender, meditate, to remove ignorance
And to be still in happiness, no special place is needed.

## Light Comes to Us

There comes a time invited or not
When you leave everything behind.
It is merging with yourself, detachment from all else.

But unseen it is a merging with everything else.
Because of the connections not seen,
It is the final removal of darkness,
So the light is seen everywhere.

## More can be Less

The more you know, the more you know you don't know.
The more effort, the less effort is required until there is none.
The more you see, the more you see there is nothing to see.
The more you hear, the more you hear nothing to hear.


## Great People

I have been in the presence of some good people,
Perhaps some of them were great people.
I have come across the traces left by others
Who perhaps were great people.

Simplicity is often a sign there may be greatness.
Humility is another sign
But compassion is the energy of the great
Whilst getting on with their work.


## Inner Self

I like people for their hearts, not for their thoughts.
You can call it the 'inner self,'
Anything you like but that is what I like.
Minds are like machines, varied, sometimes impressive
But they cannot just be the inner self.


## Unhappy Reason

How do I forget to remind myself to be happy,
Because I forget to be happy all the time?
There is no reason other than reason getting in the way.

## Bliss

I have moments sometimes lasting seconds or minutes,
Rarely all morning or afternoon,
When everything in my life is perfect,
Not a single thing is wrong.

These moments can be created if I want them by not thinking,
I have to remind myself to choose them,
And be in inner happiness.


## Days of Great Peace

On Saturday afternoons I sensed the joy
Before Sunday's solemnity,
Fun before the serious thoughts ready for the week of work.

In some places there are no weekends,
No particular days to the week,
No holidays, holy days on or off days, just days of great peace.

## 39. OUR OWN WAY

### Congratulations You are in a Mess

Congratulations because the pain and suffering are almost over
And you will be transformed.
What a relief and time to be thankful.

### Perfect

They don't tell us we are perfect,
Better than machines ever can be?
We can do much of what they do, only slower,
But they cannot be what we are; consciousness.

Why are we not told we are perfection
As we need all of our mistakes and flaws to learn?
Without them we would not have our polarity and be perfect.

### Your Own Path

You have to go your own way, straying off paths from others;
Strong enough to be on your own,
With enough fear to keep you alert.

### Your Default

Your default should be set to be kind.
Your default should be set to trust.
Your default should be set to help.
Your default may be misplaced, incorrect, fooled
But your default is always the best option for you.

## Where is Happiness

I didn't follow the usual path of one job and a pension.
I didn't invest in real estate, a holiday home or rentals.
I didn't invest in collections or anything I could sell.

I tried to find happiness simply in myself,
Even if it meant looking foolish.
Switched off about the world and its affairs,
I found happiness is our nature but not in the world.


## No Apology

Perhaps I could be criticised for having feelings which I show.
Yes I sometimes wear my heart on my sleeve
But usually when I choose to.

Maybe I could be criticised for looking inside
To know my own self,
Being in solitude detached from the world
To experience happiness there.


## Psychoanalysis

The psychoanalyst said I had fear of abandonment.
Who hasn't?
I thought.

My parent's past history was never enquired about,
Yet their history made me what I was,
So I decided psychoanalysis was intellectual and not real.

I cancelled my appointments,
But he kept on writing to me saying I could do well.
I was well, I am well.

## Oxford

I thought there would be some time for the spirit
But there was none.
It was all about thought, almost perfect thought.

Too much concern for the mind and none for the spirit,
So I turned on my heels
And found my own way.

## From Dreams

When you don't want to go
The way of your father with the addiction
Or the way of your brother with dishonesty,
You have to look somewhere else rather than up to people.
Looking sideways or leapfrogging over things,
Even to another country,
Can give you a sense of something you could not see,
Which now you can change from being just a dream.

## Returning to Inside

In trying to return to the place inside
Where I am happy and authentic,
I have to ask a question to try and rescue me.
I have to ask 'Who am I, What am I?'

Only after I ask this inside, I find the place where I just am.
Calm, still, serene I see there are no words for being this.
Continuing to stay here is a desire,
But then I see I am here all the time
I am here; just the body busy is doing other things.

## Self Food

Knowledge feeds the brain but doesn't feed the self
Because the self cannot be nourished only seen.
It needs to be able to just be. It needs us to be still.

## Longing

Why do we create longing for happiness?
Why do we dedicate most of our thinking
Longing for happiness which we already have today inside us.
Why do we long for something
Which is already ours, which is inside?

## Experience

I wish someone had left me notes, notes about what to avoid.
About being quiet and not broadcasting my thoughts.
About being happy with what we have today.
About being happy with what we hear
Rather than with what we say.
If they had, would I have learnt this as well as broadcasting?

## Notes

Why didn't people leave notes
To write about what is most important in life.
Why didn't they say how to be happy,
Instead of commandments saying what we shouldn't do?

Why didn't they say the point of life is to be happy in yourself,
Not to make others happy or to accumulate material things.
Not to be thought of. Not to be thought of as clever.
Why don't people leave notes saying how to be happy inside?

## Here Now

Maybe we don't want things to be how they were.
We only want to be how we are.
Maybe we don't want things to be better in the future.
We only want to be how we are.


## Inner Sight

Words are only words, an expression.
Words do not describe decent people well enough.
Words do not describe indecent people helpfully enough.

The eye sees, The heart sees
And the body truthfully tries to tell us what words cannot.


## Second Sight

Everyone thinks you have lost the plot
By ignoring the masterplan they think you should be living by.
Compared to their standing in the world you are not a threat.

Then the unexpected appears in their life.
What was meaningless becomes the most important.
From standing above you their only desire
Is to try and be happy sitting with you.


## Your room

Your room where you slept. Your room where you played.
Your room where you studied.
Your room where you were with friends.
Your room where you now sleep. Your room where you work.
Your room where you relax is only inside you.

## How Long?

We have to sit on a mess until we get so fed up with it,
We are so uncomfortable we have to move.


## Here

I was there when the fire nearly engulfed you forever.
I was there when you left hospital. I was there.

I was there when you were in the accident.
I was there when your friend died. I was there.

I was there when you realised your ignorance.
I was there when you realised the truth. I was there.

I will be there when you die.
I will be there after you die. I will be there.


## Hope and Fear Light and Dark

I am not usually happy to see the sun set
Because a day has nearly gone,
So there is always some fear of what the night may bring.

But I am always glad to see the sun rise
Because I am still here full of hopeful expectancy,
A true morning person.


## How Much?

How are we torn apart? How do we unfold?
How do we unbox?
How can we put us back together?

## Not Ok but Happy

How could I know I would turn out like this
Because years ago this is not what I expected my life to be like?
Years ago I would not have seen me being happy with this
But when I look back, I now see that all along,
I have been the happiest I could have been.


## Our Own Final Path

What leads you on your path may also lead another,
But for some it might be impossible.
Others may take a path which would be impossible for you.

All along, all paths lead to the same final path,
Which is the path of happiness found in stillness.
Whether in solitude or with other, we find it on our own.


## Happiness of Unhappiness

To be spiritually fit you need to be motivated
Either to be like someone in happiness of what they are,
Or to get away from how unhappy you are.
Whichever way leads you is your own path.


## How Known?

How much can you know yourself?
At what time in your life do you know yourself?
How long does it take to know yourself?
Is there an end to knowing yourself?

## Fitness

Keeping spiritually in touch is keeping spiritually fit.
Fitness needs time, effort and practice.
Spiritual fitness means being on the right spiritual diet,
Being with people on the same final path, nurturing each other.

Being in the right place in our self is everything.
But because the world is packed with others who may need us,
We need to be fit enough to move inwards all the time.


## Inner Finishing School

Whilst we are still childish, we cannot deal with life.
Whilst we are emotionally too sensitive,
We cannot relate on all levels.
Whilst we lack humility, we cannot learn.
Whilst we are in denial, we cannot change.


## Full Consciousness

As I write this time is running out.
I am spending my time like this
Because it makes me happy to enjoy myself.

Conscious of what I have got,
Why would I want to be doing anything else
Which would distract me from happiness,
Unless it is sharing it?

## Until The End

We don't understand some stories until before the end,
Just as our lives may not reveal our story until the end.
A search for meaning may not be seen until then.


## The Trace Left Behind

When you give up everything about something,
Eventually you see crystal clear why you held on to it,
No matter what trace there is left behind to remind you of it.


## On Our Own

We only find out we are on our own
When we find our self on our own,
Without support from family or friends around.

Where we might have expected sadness,
We see being on our own is being in control of our happiness.

Purpose is where we may have not have seen one.
On our own is being more connected to everyone.


## Where Happiness is now.

Always strive for nothing.
In nothing is the fullness of stillness.
In the fullness of stillness is everything.

## 40. ACCEPTANCE

### Accepting Thankfully

We can think a lot about many things,
Of others and where we are.
But at some stage we see we have to embrace it, so we need to
find acceptance.

Acceptance is not just taking what is offered
But welcoming what is offered as a gift.
The harder it is to accept, the more welcome it should be.

Acceptance is not about receiving anything,
But discovering inside us
What we need to accept and being thankful about us.

### Rehearsal

You don't often get the chance
To rehearse how to respond to bad news.
Just in case it is bad news, this is such an occasion.

Denial then nausea. Anger and disappointment.
Acceptance, acceptance and more acceptance.

### Alternatives to Truth

The true meaning even if spelt out and illustrated
Is not accepted.
Instead euphemisms, metaphors, mysteries and stories
Are nearly always preferred to truth.

## To Be Your Self

Suffering is not an option
Because it is handed to you on a plate which you have to eat.
There is no choice about receiving it or about acceptance.

Suffering breaks a part of you down again
If that part has been rebuilt since the last suffering.
It is suffering's nature as is your nature to be yourself.


## I Accept the Day

Whatever the day brings I accept it because it has been given
And it has to be lived through,
Even if it has been given to reject.


## My Deteriorating Mind

I know my memory is a little bit worse than two years ago.
Once or twice a week I can't remember some words
But because I am immersed and don't value them,
I let them go.

Not having to build up any more, being able to let go,
Accepting the state I have always been in
Is only present for me now.


## Grateful for Being Thankful

I am so grateful that I am thankful to difficulties.
I don't have to be ungrateful, resentful or envious.
But being thankful cures it of any negativity
And helps to completely accept difficult times.

## Accept

There is always a way out of every situation.
Even being blocked may be the only way out,
Which has to be accepted.


## Changing the Unchangeable

When we are in a painful place,
Sometimes it seems there is no way out.
It seems there is no alternative but to wait and accept it.

In accepting that we can't change things,
Acceptance changes us.
Only then do we see things differently.


## Happy In Sunset

Just now the sun disappeared below the horizon
And it is still very light and dusk will be here soon.

Acceptance of inevitable darkness
Makes me turn up the light inside me.

With one sunset or a hundred years of them,
Are we wiser, happier, fulfilled
Or are we the same as we were with the first one?


## Like a Flower

We think we will change.
We think things will change and improve, not knowing,
Like a flower, which can't become anything but a flower,
We also can't become anything other than what we are.

## Near retirement

In my twenties I hoped I could do the work
It is only now nearly at the end of my work
That at last I know I can do the work,
But a tiredness has entered me simply from the wear and tear.

Earlier on in youth there is no wear and tear.
So the journey of work seems easy and smooth.
But the wear and tear of age make it seem like
More effort is needed to feel good about routine things.

## The Old Hand

The amount you can do and you want to do reach a peak,
Then irreversible decline begins.
There may be productive times with great effort,
But gone is the leisurely brush of the hand.

There is little time left,
Less willingness of the brain cells to work.
Everything of value has already been gathered in,
So the hand is more desperate.
But then it relaxes as we see it is the same hand.

## Acceptance and Adjustment

We have to pick ourselves up and carry on
In whatever form we find we have become.
We may not have the desired resources,
But find we have more resolve.

## Acceptance is Happiness

Acceptance of today,
As it is, as it changes develops and ends.
Acceptance of yourself
As you are, as you change develops and ends.
Acceptance of someone,
As they are, as they change develops and ends.
Acceptance of the world,
As it is, as it changes develops and ends.
Acceptance of today, yourself, someone and the world
Is all there is.


## My Triggers

My faulty triggers are so many only a few can be mentioned.
Like having a short fuse, getting angry and raising my voice,
Perfectionism, having expectations of others and me,
Not liking criticism, not taking orders, other's forgetfulness,
Not being reciprocal, being thick skinned,
Frustration at being too soft,
Not able to reel my neck in, being wrong,
Being sad, being sentimental and being too self-critical.


## Only Acceptance

We can't change what was given to us by nature,
But we can change how we nurture it.
We can't change what has passed,
But we can change our attitude to it.
We can't change another person, only accept them.

## Choiceless path

I can't stop the inner self.
I obey its commands simply because I surrendered.
Seeing what the world is like,
There is no choice to remain there,
Surrendering is a choiceless path.

## Heart of Me

Some get their excitement from the speed of things,
Others from being so relaxed. I've never been that way.
I get my happiness from being inside.

Being on fire inside comes from nowhere.
There is a need to express it in the stillness of meditation,
Sometimes in words,
Either way it is the expression of the heart.

## From the Heart Only

I gave up trying to fight writing as it is too strong for me,
So I obey its need to be expressed.

There is only one time
I am able to stop it and completely ignore it,
If it comes from the mind not the heart.

## Treacherous

Treachery is something we have to be open to,
Otherwise we are closed.
Like darkness is part of light, it comes with trust.

## Dangerous Ferocious Beasts

The most dangerous ferocious animal ever to exist
Wasn't the T Rex.
It wasn't the sabre toothed tiger. It has always been us.

We are a chaotic mess,
But there is some love in the mix and hate.
You never know what you are going to get.

## We can't stop

We can't work anything out. We can't stop our torture.
We can't stop our violence. We can't stop our unfairness.
We can't stop our unkindness. We can't stop our thinking.
We can't stop what we can't stop

## Our Subjective True Life

Something you see from your position with your eyes only.
It is what you see, not what others see,
Which is why we cannot in truth judge.

Truth is our truth only, everyone else has their truth too.
We cannot know anyone else's truth, only ours.

## Variables

Some things take ten minutes, some less than one.
Some can never be completed in words
Because they can't be thought or written,
They can only be experienced.

## Unseen Meaning

This commentary on the spending and passing of a life
Is not an attempt to give it any meaning,
Only to show what it doesn't mean.
Then it might be easier for you to see your own meaning.

When half a dozen generations have come after us,
Our presence is no longer felt
Because no one has a living memory of us.
It seems we are gone from other's life experience.

But we do not peak during life or after it
In words, in pictures or anything we leave for others.
What we give and leave to others
Is the thread of life itself for them to pass on.

## Doubt

There comes a time where there is no doubt.
When all else is given up, doubt is unknown.

## Maintaining the Status Quo

Not accepting things in the past and still unshakable,
We can survive without all the comforts offered.
With our sight and hearts still, we can be unencumbered.

## Nothing to Do

Apart from maintaining basic body functions,
Keeping thoughts repelled
By the desire to be conscious of stillness,
Is the direct route to inner happiness.

## Accepted

We look for all sorts of reasons for why we are like this,
Our parents, our country, our school and our town,
But it cannot be worked out.
When we are limping and disabled
We don't need to be worked out.
We need support and help and to be accepted.


## Mind Control

How can these thoughts be stopped?
How can they stop bothering me so I can be in control?
Mind control is the only answer because it cures
Most mental health problems, states of all kinds of distress.
Suffering is stopped by stopping thoughts.


## Honest Now

I will be patient and I will just be me for good now.
No more dishonesty to me from me.
I will try being simply clear, even with all the hesitation.


## Be Still or Leave

Sometimes writing can simply be none other than an attempt
To let the mind think it has found some sense of order
From the chaos that appears as its reality,
Simply due to thoughts.

This is an attempt to lull thoughts
Into believing they are important,
With some meaning to them when there is none,
Other than to stop them and leave me in stillness.

## Joyous Acceptance

Acceptance is the hardest choice to make.
At first resistance reins but the alternative to resentment
Inevitability shows us we can have joy.


## Our Best Teachers

Challenging to the last moment,
Abusers show us our weakest points
So we can strengthen them for the next time.
So paradoxically we should thank them;
They are our best teachers of self respect.


## Bigger Power

How do some grow without support and some need so much?
What makes us so sensitive or hard? What needs to do this?
Perhaps it is nothing to do with genetics or nurturing,
But the needs of something in us, part of us unseen.


## You Can't Make It Up

You couldn't make it up because it is life.
When you make it up, the lie loses the energy of truth,
Just as you always know when an actor is acting.
The same loss of energy is felt when
Our ignorance of believing we are the ego is uncovered.

## Groups

I don't flourish in groups. I don't work in groups.
I am solitary and prefer one to one company in all settings.
Listening to one person is complicated
As there are so many voices present who can't speak,
Who influence what the person says,
It is difficult to identify what the person wants.
Listening to a group is different
Because they all speak not listening to each other
But want to be heard as one voice
And can only have one voice or fragment.


## No Naming

When we discover something,
Why do we feel compelled to give it a name?
Why not have some things which are nameless,
Which have no words to describe them?
When we discover someone,
Why do we feel compelled to give them a name?
Why not have someone who is nameless
Whom we have no words to describe?
Do other creatures give names which fit things like we do
Or do their instincts
Of safety, food, comfort and shelter guide them?
Does the layer of words as our intelligence
Cover up our instincts
So we can pretend not to be like other creatures?
The naked truth is we are no different. We are the same.

## 41. ORDINARY

### Ordinary Aspects

Many tame lines can be read,
Then unsuspiciously out of nowhere,
Like a hidden tiger breaking cover,
Pouncing on unsuspecting prey,
A few lines knock you over and you are changed.

Who wrote it and what it said,
What it showed is not important.
It is what I would like to have said
And that can be the reason for reading.

It makes us see, it makes us think
Like a visit to a foreign culture.
Remembering, returning home we compare what we are
With what we thought we were,
Only now the ordinary becomes special.

### In Touch

What's in the News?
It is more of the same old stuff that is new,
Just because it is newer.

There is nothing new in death but what is new is a baby.
We don't get excited unless it is one of our own
But news shows us how much we are alone.

Life is more interesting than news.
Ordinary everyday people and things
Mean more than the news and touch us much more.

**Ordinary**

Ordinariness is something envied, because
When the basic simple things are done and appreciated,
They make us happy.


**Ordinary Things**

Ordinary things, habits and routines
Help more than the written word
Routines punctuate pain and suffering
With some ordinary normality,
So at least some normality is felt.

There is little that can reduce pain and suffering
Because going through them
Cannot be avoided to move to the next stage.

The inner refuge of stillness and silence
Can always be accessed,
So it is easier to access at the most difficult time.


**Calmness as your Friend**

When your focus goes and is lost,
Great effort is needed to seem ordinary and unperturbed.
Calmness is the only path.
Hysteria, depression or anger are alternatives.

## Depth of Meaning

To have meaning is to have purpose,
Although it can be anything.
When it involves others it seems to have more meaning,
But it is the same, as it is just about us.


## Choppers

Sometimes when I need fresh inspiration,
I just go to the bathroom and clean my choppers.
What's that got to do with being inspired?
Like most places beginning with the letter B such as
Beach, bed, bath, it is probably the best place to be inspired.


## Presentation

Describing important things, events of my daily life
Is more difficult with each decade.

Things which I used to describe and report
Are now not as exciting as the ordinary.

The ordinary has been transformed into the authentic,
Now full of meaning for me.

There is no single reason why nature, beauty
And what is done and said seem more vibrant
And the sounds are louder on my ear drum.
I have become more sensitive
To all ordinary presentations to the senses.

## Here Now - No Past No Future

Your whole life so far was all about bringing you here,
Now, right now so you could see yourself.

Every happening, every journey, every failure and success,
Everything you hoped for,
Was only ever to bring you here now.

That you got here, that you are here now,
Means you can never ever leave.

Once you have seen this moment,
You don't bother with the past or future.


## Easy Street

There is no such thing as an easy life
And easy street doesn't mean life is easy.

Easy can mean no work because there is money,
But every day has to have meaning,
A single purpose with yourself.

We will always search for meaning because it is everything.
Searching for easy street is not being interested in yourself.

∞

www.ingramcontent.com/pod-product-compliance
Lightning Source LLC
Chambersburg PA
CBHW060840280326
41934CB00007B/864